A Lady's Life in Zululand and the Transvaal During Cetewayo's Reign

MRS WILKINSON

A Lady's Life in Zululand and the Transvaal During Cetewayo's Reign

The Experiences of a Missionary
in 19th Century South Africa

Annie Margaret (Green) Wilkinson

LEONAUR

A Lady's Life in Zululand and the Transvaal During Cetewayo's Reign
The Experiences of a Missionary in 19th Century South Africa
by Annie Margaret (Green) Wilkinson

First published under the titles
A Lady's Life in Zululand and the Transvaal During Cetewayo's Reign

Leonaur is an imprint of Oakpast Ltd

Copyright in this form © 2012 Oakpast Ltd

ISBN: 978-0-85706-838-5 (hardcover)
ISBN: 978-0-85706-839-2 (softcover)

http://www.leonaur.com

Contents

Preface   9

Departure From England and Arrival in Africa   11

Tarrying in Natal   21

The Start For Zululand, and First Impressions   34

Great Annual Review of the Zulu Army by Panda
and Cetywayo   46

Cetywayo's Way of Governing His Country; An Insight
to His 'Reign of Terror'   60

Station Life in Zululand   74

Exploring the Amaswazi Country   84

Station Life, and a Start For Amaswazi Land   95

Sickness, Famine, and the Gathering of the Zulu War
Storm   109

In the Transvaal, and On the Bombo   124

Incidents of Native Christians   143

Northward of Zululand   154

Journeyings in the Transvaal   165

Results of Mission Work as Seen Through the Zulu War   174

To the dear memory of
A woman of rare virtues
High-minded and guileless
The sharer of every joy, the sympathiser in
Every sorrow
In journeyings often the faithful and never-failing
Companion
In every relation of domestic and public life
The best friend
And
The wisest counsellor
That the compiler of this memoir ever had
Or ever will have

The Lord gave, and the Lord hath taken away;
blessed be the name of the Lord

Preface

The letters composing this *Memoir* are published with a view to giving an idea of the kind of life which a lady is called upon to live when she leaves her English home for the purpose of aiding in the extension of Christ's kingdom in such a wild and savage country as Zululand. There are few persons who can realise what such a life entails, nor can letters written even upon the spot convey any adequate idea of it.

The letters here published are, like her who wrote them, so simple and unaffected, and describe the experiences of Zulu life in a style so unconscious of troubles cheerfully met, and hardships bravely endured, that they must carry the strength of truth with them, and do good wherever they are read. That they may stir others to do and to dare what this brave and unselfish Englishwoman did and dared so willingly for Christ's sake—in journeyings often, in perils of waters, in perils by the heathen, in perils in the wilderness; in weariness and painfulness, in watchings often, in hunger and thirst, in sickness and in loneliness; besides those things which came upon her daily, the care of young and tender children—is the sole reason that they are now given to the public.

Caerhayes, Cornwall:
July 1882.

CHAPTER 1

Departure From England and Arrival in Africa

On July 6, 1870, Mrs. Wilkinson, the author of these letters, sailed from Falmouth, with the Mission party bound for Zululand, in the *Good Hope*. On the 13th she wrote these few lines from Madeira:—

> Just one line to tell you of our safe arrival at this most beautiful of islands. We anchored here at eleven last night, in the midst of a total eclipse of the moon. The town lies at the bottom of such a splendid mountain, dotted all over with cottages and vine-yards. I have been very ill all the time, or I would have written more. We are now going on shore to breakfast. We had two nice services on Sunday, by your time 11 a.m. and 8.45 p.m., ship's time 10.15 a.m. and 7.45 p.m. I cannot write more.

After leaving Madeira she wrote a description of her short stay upon that island. It shows the keen interest she took in everything, and the keen delight with which she enjoyed every bright day and hour of life. It was always *carpe diem* with her. Ever patient and uncomplaining in the darkest and most troubled days, of which she had in Africa not a few; ever hopeful that light would come again when the dark days had done their work, and set all things to rights. *Go, sleep like closing flowers at night, and heaven thy morn will bless*, was the atmosphere in which, like the flowers, she lived, and moved, and had her being. She was a very bad sailor, and always felt wretched on board ship. To make matters worse, the *Good Hope* was a rolling and most uncomfortable ship, deeply laden, very slow, and ended by her engines breaking down before Capetown was reached. Little was made, however, of the many and prolonged discomforts, as will be seen in the following letter, complaining never; it was not in her nature to do so.

Good Hope. Sunday, July 24, 1870.
Lat. 2; long. 12.

You will now be about receiving my scrap from Madeira. I will go back to that time. It is one of the most charming places I ever saw. We went on shore about 7.30 a.m., and on landing found a quaint little covered *sledge*, drawn by two oxen, waiting, into which we got and went to the English hotel, where we had a most delicious breakfast, with quantities of fruit, which I can tell you we thoroughly enjoyed after a week of sickness. After breakfast we went to see some gardens. And now, how can I describe them to do them justice? It was like wandering through hot-houses, with a beautiful sea breeze blowing all the time; we could but keep saying to each other, "Paradise must be like this." Home flowers we came upon at each turn, growing under magnificent palms. To show you what the growth is, there was an English oak sixty-seven years old, and ten feet six inches round the trunk.

It was terrible leaving this peaceful spot to come back to this horrible old "roller." I have been ill the whole time; but today I feel better, so take advantage and begin a letter to be posted at St. Helena. We cross the line tomorrow. We have been most favoured; instead of being scorched we have had winds and cloudy skies, and at this moment I can hardly keep my paper quiet. The captain says he never crossed the line in such cool weather; but we are. so deep in the water that until today we have not had our cabin ports open for a week, so you can imagine the state of atmosphere below.

We are so pleased with all our party. Only fancy, I find that the person who comes half as my helper, half as worker in the Mission, is Miss B., who came and started the orphanage at Foxearth, and you can guess how many Foxearth talks we have.

Saturday, July 30.—We hope to get to St. Helena tomorrow night. It has been a weary time since we left Madeira, and this is a very slow ship; we ought to have been at St. Helena yesterday. We have seen a good many flying-fish. I had one for lunch; it was most delicious, something between a whiting and an eel. We ought to arrive at Cape town eleven days after we leave St.

Helena, and then we shall have about seven days up to Durban. I think this life on board has been a good preparation for our future life; everything will seem to be such a comfort on shore. We ought to be so thankful that we have not had one really hot day; always a cool breeze, though a head wind.

We horrify those accustomed to it (*i.e.* the colonists) by not admiring the Southern Cross. It looks to me like a boy's kite. The meals on board are as follows:—Coffee or tea 6 a.m., breakfast 9 a.m., lunch 12, dinner 4 p.m., tea 7 p.m. There was a man in irons all yesterday for knocking the engineer into the stokehole. The sun now sets at 5.45 p.m., and it is quite dark by 6 p.m. We are in lat. 13. I never expected to be ill the whole voyage, which I now see plainly I shall be. I am the only person allowed to have my meals on deck.

Sunday, July 31.—I must finish this letter today, as we hope to arrive at St. Helena at six this evening. We had a nice service this morning, with celebration—the second time on board. Everybody is in spirits at the thought of sighting land. We passed a vessel this morning, the first we have seen for eighteen days.

The next letter is from Bishop's Court, Capetown, where the Mission party stayed a few days. The Bishop of Capetown had gone to England with Mrs. Gray to consult with English doctors upon her state of health. It was their last visit. Mrs. Gray returned to South Africa almost immediately, and lived but a short while after her return. In their absence the Mission party were hospitably entertained at Bishop's Court by the Miss Grays.

Bishop's Court, Capetown. Aug. 16, 1870.
You will hear, before this reaches you, that the Metropolitan has gone to England with his wife, who is very ill. The news met us at St. Helena, and, as you can well imagine, we were astonished. It was most unfortunate our missing him at that place. He left it on the Friday, the day we ought to have arrived there, but did not until the Monday. We had a long, tedious voyage from St. Helena here, being four days longer than we ought to have been, owing to our engines continually breaking down, and having to stop three or four hours at a time, and sometimes six, to repair them. We dropped anchor in Table Bay on Sunday morning at 1.45 a.m. We came on shore at 8 a.m., and went to the hotel for breakfast.

We had not been there half-an-hour before poor E. got a letter asking him to preach in the cathedral at the 11 o'clock service. Was it not too bad to attack a poor seasick man in that manner? We enjoyed the service immensely—such good singing and full cathedral service. It is the only colonial cathedral where a cathedral service is carried out. Directly service was over the Precentor, Canon Ogilvie, brought us out here about nine miles from town. Bishop Gray had arranged everything for us, and here we are in a charming old Dutch house, such large lofty rooms, and polished oak floors, a beautiful garden in the middle of a little park, and on one side Table Mountain rising straight above our heads. Beautiful grey granite, with here and there patches of grass, and forests of firs.

The weather in the early morning before breakfast, when E. and I take a stroll, is like a lovely October morning in England—heavy dew on the grass, and slightly frosty. We go into the kitchen garden and pick a couple of delicious oranges. After the grove of oranges and lemons you come to peas and cabbages on one side, and a grove of standard apricots and peaches—which are now bare of leaf—on the other. At the bottom a running stream full of watercresses.

Yesterday we went for a drive in the morning, and in the afternoon went up the mountain on a fern expedition. The ferns are magnificent; E. is going to send a parcel of them home by one of the officers of the ship. You shall have some from Zululand. The everlastings are not yet out. In the evening, clergy and their wives to meet E. at dinner. The Miss Grays are so nice and kind, doing everything they can to make us comfortable. I cannot realise yet that I am in Africa; I am too comfortable. We are to go on board tomorrow at 3 p.m. We shall be about three days getting to Algoa Bay, where we stay three days. The Bishop of Grahamstown comes down to meet us. What do you think the Metropolitan and the other Bishops want E. to do? To land at Algoa Bay, and go on a visitation to the Free State and Transvaal country.

The Archdeacon here, the Metropolitan's commissary, is very anxious he should go. At breakfast they were discussing it very gravely. E. was saying that his own diocese required him first, and that he ought to settle our party down there. So when the Archdeacon said, "It is so much easier to get to the Free State

14

from Grahamstown than from Zululand," I made them all burst out laughing by saying, "Then why does not the Bishop of Grahamstown go himself?" On Sunday evening we went down to service at Claremont, close to Rondebosch.

From Capetown the Mission party proceeded by sea to Port Elizabeth, where a few pleasant days were spent with a hospitable member of the Church, Mr. Alfred Ebden, and where the Bishop of Grahamstown, now Bishop of Edinburgh, was met, having come a journey of ninety miles for that special purpose. From here also a letter was written home.

Port Elizabeth, Algoa Bay. Aug. 23, 1870.

Here we are another stage on our journey, and I sincerely hope we shall soon be at the end of the sea part of it. We go on board tomorrow, and I hope on Friday, the 26th, we shall get to Durban. We are staying in the house of a Mr. Ebden, a friend of the Bishop of Grahamstown, who has come down ninety miles to meet as. Have you heard that he has been offered the Bishopric of Edinburgh, and he is going to accept it? He will be a *terrible* loss to South Africa, for he commands the respect of *all* parties. He was the moving spirit at the late *synod*. I do not know what the Bishop of Capetown will do without him.

Everybody is going mad on the subject of diamonds, as they are really turning out something more than a snare and a delusion. One has been found which surpasses the Kohi-noor in brilliancy, though not in size. Mr. Ebden showed us several last night varying from 50*l.* to 300*l.* in value. They are found about three feet from the surface of the ground in the bed of an old river. They have been found upon an old mission station, and the missionaries allowed the diggers to work on condition that they should have a seventh. In one week their share was 1,000*l.* If E. goes up there, which I think he must do at the end of the year, I tell him that he must dig a little, for he will go through the thick of it.

As I sit by the window writing, waggons keep passing, with twelve or fourteen oxen drawing them, but I have not yet seen the sort of waggon we shall go in. These are entirely for goods. E. preached twice on Sunday. There are three churches here, and the people are thoroughly English; there is not the mixture of Dutch which you find at the Cape.

15

We left Capetown last Wednesday. It was blowing hard, and in the night it blew quite a gale against us, so that we had only gone about fifty miles the first twenty-four hours. I only hope the wind will keep in its present quarter, and we shall soon run up to Durban.

E. paid his first visit to a *Kafir kraal* (village) yesterday; and though one has heard of the *Kafir* absence of dress, still, he says, he was not prepared for it. The children had literally nothing on, and the men simply a blanket, which sometimes was on and sometimes off. What a lot of letters you will have had from us, and we, poor things, are hungering for one, and I know not when we shall hear! There are a good many English flowers here: a large bouquet is by me consisting of verbena, mignonette, stock, wallflower.

After I finished my last letter to you, written from Bishop's Court, we drove to Constantia, the great wine place. We saw fields of vines; they look like a quantity of closely-trimmed gooseberry-bushes, not growing at all like hops, but kept quite short. We bought two nine-gallon casks of wine to take up with us. It was a most beautiful drive: Table Mountain towering above us on one side; in the distance the Blue Mountains of Hottentot Holland, the tops covered with snow; and in front the sea. We have already found out how clear and light the air is, and we have day after day without a cloud. I hope you are having equally lovely weather, though they say that the quantity of S.E. wind we have had will bring you rain.

We lunched with the sisters at the Home at Capetown before we went on board; we also went over the *Kafir* college at Zonnebloem, and saw our three Zulu boys, Hali, Billy, and Charlie. They are three such nice, intelligent lads, much handsomer than dear old Frank.[1] Billy looks almost like an English boy. I think his father was English. The English college at Rondebosch is very nice; the headmaster a charming man, who keeps the boys well up to all English sports. It will be just the place for T. when he is about eleven years old. One of the masters has just come back from England, having gained the Hebrew scholarship at Oxford.

What we miss most are the English singing-birds. Now and

---

1. An Ajawa from Lake Nyassa, placed in Mrs. Wilkinson's charge in England by Bishop Tozer of Zanzibar.

then we hear a bird piping beautifully, but there is no song.

Bishop Cotterill's daughter, Mrs. Greenstock, lives next door. She has been living for ten years in as secluded a spot as Kwamagwaza, so that I gain many hints. They were obliged to leave at last, as the neighbourhood was not healthy; but she says that they were so happy there, and her husband's work was so successful. They are hoping soon to go home for a holiday, and are only here filling a clergyman's place who is at home. There is now a fortnightly mail to Natal (instead of monthly). It leaves England the 9th and 24th, so you must write as often as possible. It has only been started this year. Did you think of us on the 18th? We were both so ill, as the gale was blowing; but we drank each other's health in *porter*, which is the only thing that does me good.

The next letter announces the arrival of the Mission party at Durban, after a voyage of nearly two months, instead of twenty-four days in which the run is now made from Plymouth to Natal.

Durban, Natal. Aug. 29, 1870.

Here we are, I am very thankful to say, at the end of our voyage, and most hospitably received by Archdeacon Robinson and his wife, while the rest of our party are at the hotel. We anchored in the bay yesterday morning (Sunday) at 7 a. m.; but we were not able to land, the sea ran too high over the bar across which we had to go in cargo-boats. It was most tantalising having to spend another day and night on the ship when we had all come up dressed in *full fig* to go ashore. However, today, about 12, we espied a boat coming to us, for we lay three miles from the landing-place. We were all packed closely down in the cargo-boat with the luggage, and they prepared to batten us down for going over the bar; but we begged and prayed not to be suffocated in that manner, and they did not, and we did not get wet. The country strikes us as being the most inhabited part of Africa we have seen since Capetown itself; well cultivated, with plenty of houses, and the land rises well from the sea. Durban itself is very low, being only about one foot above the level of the sea. The coast from Algoa Bay up here is very lovely, though not a house to be seen, unless an occasional *Kafir* hut might be called one. Such beautiful wooded heights, waterfalls, and rivers running into the sea.

It was found impossible, for several reasons, that the Mission party should go up at once to Zululand. One reason was that house accommodation was not prepared, and the rainy season was commencing, which rendered it necessary that the ladies of the party should at once be properly housed. After a week, therefore, spent in Durban, during which stores were laid in, and waggons started off for Kwamagwaza in Zululand—which was to be, at all events for a time, the headquarters of the newly arrived Mission party—Mrs. Wilkinson went up to Maritzburg, where she became for a time the guest of Dean Green, and, later on, of the Bishop of Maritzburg.

The Deanery, Pieter Maritzburg. Sept. 8, 1870.
We landed in Durban last Monday week, the 29th. On Tuesday, Wednesday, Thursday, and Friday we were busy from 10 a.m. to 5 p.m. shopping. The two young men of the Mission party, Mr. Glover and Mr. Hales, went off upon the last-named day with four waggons. On Saturday we had a quiet day, settling accounts, &c. On Sunday E. preached morning and evening. Monday we had to "return calls." On Tuesday E. started me off in the omnibus at 6.30 a.m. for this place. He was to start at 9 a.m. with the Archdeacon to ride into Zululand. The Archdeacon was going with him as far as the Tugela River, the boundary of the colony, and half-way to Kwamagwaza. There he was to pick up the waggons and meet Mr. Robertson. They were to be there last night, which would be two days from Durban, and they would have two days' more ride before reaching Kwamagwaza.
E. would then just settle the young men, and set them to work, go and visit the king, and ride back here to me. I hope he will return about the 20th. It is fifty-six miles from Durban here. I came half-way on Tuesday. Bishop Macrorie most kindly drove his own nice little carriage to meet me. We all slept at the little, clean inn, and then the next morning started at 7 a.m. and got here about 2 p.m. The scenery between this and Durban is simply magnificent. We were about 3,000 feet high, and surrounded with hills.
Of course the road is rather alarming sometimes to one fresh from Suffolk—the way we rattled down the hills! but then the horses are accustomed to it. I could not bear Durban; the place is on a level with the sea, and the air is so hot and heavy. The streets are all sand; it is just like walking across that heavy piece

of sand at Yarmouth. We both agreed that we could not live there. Here the air is so different, so light and easy to breathe, and they tell us that the air is even clearer in Zululand.

On Sunday we had a heavy thunderstorm with hail, which lay round the church six inches deep, and was there twenty-four hours after. The moon is now full, and so bright that we might read by it. It is a perfect evening, so cool and delicious, but then we are 2,500 feet above the sea. The *Kafir* school is in the garden. I have just been listening to them singing a hymn in *Kafir* to the tune, "How sweet the Name of Jesus sounds."

We were so glad to leave the *Good Hope*. I only took one meal down below the whole voyage. I was as bad the last day I spent on board as I was the first,

Everybody is leaving this place for the diamond fields, which are turning out something very tangible, I hope the Bishop of Capetown will bring out a bishop for the Free State, for then E. won't have to go up there. It is now just 2 o'clock here, with you 12 (midday); and the thermometer is only 66° in my bedroom, which faces west.

It may be imagined that 'a quiet day, settling accounts' is necessary after purchasing stores for, and packing them in, four South African waggons for upcountry journey. To give some idea of what is required for African travel, here are items furnished to me by the late well-known African traveller, Mr. Baines:—

Equipment for one waggon, and party of three white men, and three natives, to the River Zambesi.

Waggon; twenty oxen; gear; tent.

Provisions.—Three *muids* Boers' meal; 100 lbs. flour; 200 lbs. sugar; 150 lbs. coffee, roasted and ground; six quartern chests tea; 100 lbs. salt; spices; vinegar; pepper; mustard, &c.

Medicines,—Four boxes of wine and spirits; six ounces of quinine; tartar emetic; opium; Livingstone pills; Dover's powders; ammonia; arnica; lint; adhesive plaister.

Guns and ammunition.—One or two good rifles; one or two good shot-guns; half-a-dozen muskets; 200 lbs. powder; 10,000 caps; 400 lbs. lead and shot.

Barter goods.—Four hundred pounds of beads; 60 blankets; 50 cotton blankets; 25 pieces of stout calico; 25 pieces Voerchitz (chintz); 200 handkerchiefs; box of butcher's knives; tinder boxes; strike-fire knives; 100 lbs. brass wire.

Accessories.—Three saws; three American axes; three small *ditto*; augers from half to one and a half inch; chisels; hammers; screws; nails; bolts and nuts; sewing needles and twine; thread; tape; palm and sail needles; buttons; padlocks and two keys; buckets; spades; kettles; frying pans; knives, forks, and plates; *Kafir* cooking pots; cups and pannikins; cooking gear of other and all needed sorts.

CHAPTER 2

Tarrying in Natal

The Deanery, Maritzburg. Sept. 18, 1870.
I can hardly realise that I am in Africa. Everything is so English, and it is only when I am rudely awakened by seeing a *Kafir* in the garb alone that Nature gave him that I am aware of the fact. The scenery is very fine—such hills, and such roads! I don't think you would like being rattled down a hill, much steeper than the slope down to your river, more than I do. When I drove here with the Bishop of Maritzburg I held on grimly, and did not breathe till we were at the bottom of the hill.
E. left me at Durban; he rode to Kwamagwaza with his waggons and two young men. He intended settling them, and then riding back to me here. It is about 140 miles, and it will take him four days. The waggons only travel twenty miles a day. They are drawn by fourteen oxen, and the mattresses are placed on the top of the boxes.

September 22.—E. arrived here on the 20th, after having ridden 300 miles in the fortnight, and such riding![1]
He often had to lead his horse down a precipice where one else step might be fatal. He said that Zululand teemed with game, antelopes, and bustards, crossing the path within easy shot. At one house where he stayed they shot an alligator the night before. There are a great many in the rivers which would soon snap you up if they had the chance. E. knocked up six horses, so you can imagine how he rode. Horses are cheap; a good one

1. It will be interesting to remark here that the route lay by the Lower Tugela Drift where now stand Forts Pearson and Tenedos. Thence along the track traversed by Lord Chelmsford to relieve Colonel Pearson, by the rivers Inyoni, Amatikulu, Umsindusi, Inyezani, to Etyowe, which is half way to Kwamagwaza.

is twenty pounds.

We go today to stay with Bishop Macrorie and his wife. They have kindly asked us to make their house our own until I am well enough to go up country. We had partridges for dinner on September 8, rather larger than English birds, and more of the pheasant flavour. The season *ended* on the 15th of this month, this being the spring.

The country in Zululand is very mountainous; nothing tropical will grow, but all European fruits and vegetables. The fires on the hills every night are very grand; they burn all the grass. In about three weeks green grass springs up. We shall have to build a great deal. The changes here are sudden. Tuesday a trying hot wind, and clouds of dust; yesterday and today chilly. Everybody that can go is gone to the diamond fields.

The route to Kwamagwaza by the Lower Tugela Drift has become so intensely interesting during the present war, lying as it does by our forts on the Zulu coast and through Etyowe (not Ekowe, as usually, and wrongly, spelt), that it is thought well to give the journal of the ride referred to in the foregoing letter which Mrs. Wilkinson sent home with it:—

JOURNAL OF A RIDE FROM DURBAN TO ZULULAND,
AND BACK TO MARITZBURG.

Tuesday, September 6, 1870.—Left Durban on horseback with the Archdeacon for Zululand. Baited at Victoria. Visited Mrs. Dawes, in whose house Bishop Mackenzie, when Archbishop of Natal, held service every week for many months. This good woman speaks in terms of the deepest affection of the Bishop. He left his surplice in her charge, and nothing will induce her to part with it. She looks upon it as a sacred relic. Speaks of him as ever going about trying to do good. Tells of his adapting hymns to please his little congregation in this cottage. Saw Mount Moreland Church in the distance (one of Archdeacon Mackenzie's churches). Slept at Knox's, Umhlali.

Wednesday, September 7.—Left Knox's at daybreak, passed Umhlali Church, and "Seaforth," where the Mackenzies lived. All savours of him here. The Knoxes speak so kindly of all three, the bishop and his two sisters. Breakfasted with Mr. Addison, and looked over his sugar mill. A great bush-fire came roaring up to his sugar estate while we were here. All the *Kafirs* of the neighbourhood turned out with sticks to extinguish it. Thousands of pounds may be lost by these fires in half-an-hour. Archdeacon Robinson went to see a poor woman here who had just lost her child which he had baptised when passing here six months since. It was buried yesterday, we suppose in the garden, for there is no church nearer than the Umhlali, fifteen miles or more away. Arrived at Captain Walmesley's—the Zulu border Government Agent—about 2 p.m., where we were received very hospitably. This is a very nice house and estate; kept up well, and showing what may be done by a colonist in an out-of-the-way spot. The Archdeacon left after dinner for his visitation of the northern part of the colony.

Thursday, September 8.—Today Captain Walmesley killed an ox in honour of my arrival, and invited the Zulus on his estate to come and dance and feast. They came in great force, some three hundred, all in war attire, plumes, *assegais*, shields, &c.; a splendid lot of men, especially two young chiefs. One old chief was present who fought under Panda in days gone by. A note arrived from Glover today, who reported that the waggons reached the Tugela on Wednesday evening; river too high to cross; that Mr. Robertson was not there, and that he and Hales were in want of vegetables. Sent them a sack of sweet potatoes.

Friday, September 9.—Hales and one of the waggon drivers arrived on foot from the Tugela, wanting bread, Mr. Robertson not yet arrived from Zululand. Took leave of Captain and Mrs. Walmesley after dinner, and returned with Hales to the Tugela; arrived there at sunset. Lovely view of Tugela valley and river, with sun setting behind the blue mountains of Zululand; first view of my diocese. Was sorry to find that Myers, the waggon driver, had outspanned on the low, reedy, unhealthy ground close to the river. No signs of Mr. Robertson. What can have become of him? I begin to doubt if my messenger has reached Kwamagwaza. No room in the waggon for me to sleep, so I return two miles to a Mr. Dickens's, a coffee estate, who receives me very kindly. Just as I am getting into bed a messenger arrives from the Tugela to say that Mr. Robertson has arrived on horseback on the other (Zulu) side of the river. I am very thankful for this, for I was getting uneasy; the waggon drivers saying they could not stay beyond Monday; nowhere to stow the four waggon loads nearer than Dickens's, and a prospect, at this season, of the river rising higher any day.

Saturday, September 10.—Up at daybreak and down to Tugela; met Mr. Robertson, who had walked to meet me. Talked over plans. No time, he thought, for me to go to Kwamagwaza, having to be in Maritzburg between the 15th and 20th; certainly not, if we went by waggons. Mr. R. very anxious I should just go up, if even for a day or two, as they would be disappointed at Kwamagwaza if I did not. Resolved to ride up, and leave Glover and Hales to come on in waggons. Crossed by ferry. English people near ferry asked Mr. R. to baptise their children, others near wanting same; in all, six. Mr. R,. promised to baptise them when next down at Tugela. They ask for a few days' notice to get things clean and nice. This is very pleasant to find people still valuing the Church's sacraments when out of all reach of a clergyman and a church. This request, when setting foot in my diocese, is a very cheering one.

Rode all day to reach Norwegian Mission Station[2] (Mr. Oftebrö's). Saw many antelopes and bustards as we went along. Called at two German mission stations *en route*, and two *kraals*. Mr. R. creeps into a hut without much ceremony, and makes himself as much at home as if he were a Zulu. The cause of Mr. R.'s visit to one of these *kraals* was to see a sick old man. A sheep had run up against his leg; nothing can be done for him. Mr. B. asked the people at this *kraal* to lend him a boy to stay with him at Kwamagwaza. He had asked this here before, and this time it was granted; the boy is to go in a day or two. This is exactly what I think so wise, to get lads from all the surrounding country to Kwamagwaza for the purpose of education. If we can keep them, so much the better; they may become teachers or clergymen. If not, well, they go back and sow the seed amongst their people. As an instance of this, at one of the *kraals* we visited today we saw a boy who had been at Kwamagwaza, and been taken away again to his *kraal*. The people told us he always prayed night and morning, and prayed for them also. This is very blessed.

The last two hours of our journey was by moonlight, and over a very rough country. Glad to reach Etyowe after a hard scramble in a high wind.

Sunday, September 11—A quiet day at Etyowe. This is a very nice, tidy station, with the best church[3] in Zululand. In the churchyard lies the first Mrs. Robertson, beneath a large stone cross. She met her death near here by the upsetting of a waggon. Attended the service in church at noon. About forty natives present, all clean and well dressed, and a hearty service, in which all joined. Luther's hymns reminded me

2. Etyowe, where Colonel Pearson was shut up for so many weeks.
3. From its little tower Colonel Pearson flashed his signals to the Lower Tugela Drift, a distance of thirty-five miles.

of home. Mr. Oftebrö preached on the Gospel for the day, the "Good Samaritan." He told them of the enmity existing between Jew and Samaritan, and yet the Samaritan helped his enemy.

"Now," said Mr. Oftebrö, "if a Zulu saw one of the Amaswazi tribe in need, or dying, it would be considered right to leave him to die without helping him. This is wrong; this is not what Christ taught us." In the afternoon there was prayer in the schoolroom, and in the evening the Christians meet together, and talk over the sermon they heard in the morning.

It is very touching to think of these single-hearted Norwegians leaving their far mountains and fiords to take the Gospel to this people amongst whom they have no interest whatever beyond the love of souls. They have a little community here, builders, &c., and, having been twenty years in the country, have got things very comfortable.

★★★★★★

I must break the journal here, for a space, to state that here, on this very station, six years later fell the first Zulu martyr— soon to be followed by others—killed for his faith's sake by the cruel Cetywayo. Here, upon this very spot, three years later was an English fort; this station was an entrenched camp, God's judgement, I believe, upon, and protest against, that hard tyrant's deeds of blood with which he had defiled his land. How little I thought all that was coming upon this station as I sat about in that pleasant garden on that peaceful Sunday afternoon! The following is an account of the death of the first Zulu martyr as it reached us:—

> An *impi* (band of spearmen) came to him, saying they had orders to kill him. He asked for what reason; and on being told it was because he was a Christian, and for nothing else, he said: "Well, I rejoice to die for the Word of the Lord." He begged leave to kneel down and pray, which he was allowed to do. After praying, he said, "Kill me now." They had never seen any man act in this manner before when about to be killed, and seemed afraid to touch him. After a long pause, however, a young Zulu took a gun and shot him, and they all ran away. On the following day the people of the station were much alarmed. Zulus who were there to work left, and all the women and children were put in a place of safety, while

the men kept watch.

An *impi* was said to be gathered at Umsulu's *kraal*, not far off, and an attack was apprehended. However, the following morning (Sunday) dawned without anything of the kind. It is, however, currently reported, and believed throughout the country, that the king says the Mission stations are full of *abatakati* (witches), and that more bloodshed is imminent. When an untutored Zulu is thus able to die in the spirit and with the fortitude of a true martyr, surely we need not despair either of Christianity in South Africa, or even of the sanguinary tribes which own Cetywayo as king.

★★★★★★

Monday, September 12.—Off early to Kwamagwaza, a very rough country indeed, especially about the Umhlatuzi, very like Wales. In many places one false step would endanger life or limb. Leading one's horse down such places is not pleasant; he may come on the top of you. As we neared Kwamagwaza it was pleasant to see the bright faces and glad welcomes that greeted Mr. R. One old man said to him that it did him good to see the bishop on his way to Kwamagwaza. Arrived at Kwamagwaza towards sunset. Found Mrs. Robertson, Mr. Jackson, and Adams ready to welcome us. Attended service in the evening.

Tuesday, September 13.—Up at daybreak, then service. Mr. R. wished me to speak to the people, through him, a few words. I told them that I had come to help Mr. R. in his work; that we in England were once what they are; that missionaries came over and taught us, and we were come to teach them. I asked them to pray for me in my work amongst them, and to help the work themselves by telling the people around the good tidings they had heard, and to draw them to church. That there was only one way to be happy here and hereafter—to live good lives and to serve Christ faithfully.

Looked at a site for a church with Mr. Robertson. A very good one, on high ground away from other buildings, in case of fire, and near the burial-ground, where lies young Stokes, the boy Bishop Mackenzie brought out from the Cambridge Industrial Schools, and who was killed by a buffalo in the Zulu country. Looked round our little house, and ordered several alterations, which will make it comfortable. A long day, but a useful one, I hope; measuring and planning all day. *Began* my work by hearing a class of girls read at evening school.

Wednesday, September 14.—My horse strayed away over the hill, and I saw a neatly-dressed Christian girl bringing it back. I asked who she was. "Oh," said Mr. Robertson, " it is Agnes, the girl supported by the Walsham-le-Willows Mission army." Wasn't it strange that neither Mr. R. nor the girl, of course, knew that I was in any way connected with Walsham, and yet this almost first act of kind help done to me by a Zulu should be done by a girl supported and educated by the children of Walsham?[4]

Started immediately after morning service, with a native Christian (Joseph) as guide, for Etyowe, *en route* for Maritzburg. I had not intended leaving until Friday morning; but something seemed to urge me to get out of the Zulu country as soon as possible, as there were signs of changing weather. Angry clouds at sunset over towards the Drakensberg, a sure sign of coming rain, and if it were so it would be impossible to get over this wild, mountainous country; swollen rivers and thick weather might keep me days, and even weeks.

It was well I did leave, as what I had anticipated came to pass. All day in saddle, the faithful Joseph trudging on before, and being unable to speak to one another, it was not a lively day. On, on, on, a weary day's march. The sun rose higher, the day grew hotter. The great scarlet-winged grasshoppers, as large as humming-birds, rose as we disturbed them from the tall grass, fluttered awkwardly with a harsh rattle of their wings, and flung themselves into the grass again. Hawks wheeled round in the air, and the great, heavy African crow croaked out a sulky welcome as we passed along. Natives hoeing in their gardens looked up; some only stared, others spoke to Joseph; others from distant hill-tops and hill-sides shouted, as is their wont, at the top of their voices, which, as far as I could make out, simply meant nothing but a break in upon the silence and monotony of the scene.

Crossed the beautiful Umhlatuzi higher up than with Mr. R., and at an easier place. This river is the most beautiful piece of scenery I have come across. Off-saddled twice during the day, once by the side of a little stream fall of ferns. Here Joseph sat down and took out his Bible and read. There are not, I fear, many English labouring lads who upon a four days' journey on foot would take their Bible as a companion. I asked him the next day where he had been reading, and he opened the Bible at once at St. John's Gospel, chapter iii., and pointed to that and a few verses of chapter iv. This showed that he had not forgotten what he had read the day before.

---

4. The bishop's birthplace.

I sat and read the Psalms for the day. That magnificent seventy-second missionary psalm was one of them, from, which I had so often preached in England.

> *The mountains also shall bring peace, and the little hills righteousness unto the people. . . . His dominion shall be also from the one sea to the other, and from the flood unto the world's end. They that dwell in the wilderness shall kneel before Him, His enemies shall lick the dust. . . . All kings shall fall down before Him, all nations shall do Him service. He shall deliver their souls from falsehood and wrong, and dear shall their blood be in His sight.*

Never did those words *"falsehood and wrong"* come out so clearly as now, looking, as I did, over hill and valley dotted with the *kraals* of these poor people, given over to every kind of falsehood, every description of wrong; witchcraft, lying, divinations, superstitions of the darkest kind, foul sins and vices too filthy to name; and all these things leading to bloodshed and massacre. *"Dear shall their blood be in His sight."* It was a relief to turn and look at the young Christian at my side reading the only Book that could deliver from falsehood and wrong, which could alone show how dear His people's blood was in the sight of the righteous God. . . .

Saddled up, and off again; sun got lower, day grew cooler, the everlasting frogs in every marsh croaked out their incessant and abominable "goodnight." We now got on to the waggon track, and, fearing it might get dark before I reached Etyowe, I left Joseph to follow, and galloped on, arriving at sundown. Here again a kindly welcome at the good Norwegian's hands awaited me. Oftebrö's barometer going down steadily, and things not looking pleasant.

Thursday, September 15.—Off early for Tugela. Clouds getting up. Verily one day in this country telleth another, and so I have nothing to tell. The sun rose and made the day hotter, the scarlet grasshoppers fluttered up again and fell, the disgusting crows croaked their abominable croak, and still we trudged on till about two o'clock, when I could stand the monotony of the pace no longer. Being on the waggon track, which I thought was sufficiently well marked to prevent my losing the way, I left Joseph, and galloped on the last ten miles to the Tugela Drift.

Saw today several bucks; one sprang from a bush close to my horse's nose, and made him shy into the opposite bush, nearly putting me off. Saw also bustards, large snake-birds, and two cranes, which stalked lazily out of the path, as though they felt that they had far more right there than I. Reached Tugela Drift about 3.30 p.m. The Anglo-Dutch people on the Zulu side gave me a cup of coffee, and we chatted together about a school which they seemed very anxious should be established there for the children of the several white families, who seem wretchedly poor.[5] I asked them to let me know how many white children there were in the district, and what each family would subscribe towards building a school and supporting a teacher. This they promised to do, and seemed willing to do their best. I asked them if they would have the six children ready for baptism the following morning; if so, I would cross the Tugela, go on six miles to Captain Walmesley's, sleep there, and return for the purpose early. They said they would do their best, and get them together by 7 a.m.

I left them and crossed in the boat, a *Kafir* leading my horse, which was nearly sinking more than once in the treacherous quicksands, which are ever shifting. I had thought, in my inexperience, of crossing on his back, and was truly thankful I did not when I saw him plunging down half under the water, sometimes sinking down behind in the sandy bed till he seemed to be sitting up like a dog. Got to Captain Walmesley's at sundown, and right glad to find myself there. My horse knocked up and ill with lampas. The roof of the mouth swells in this disease, and the animal cannot eat mealies. So I left him at the captain's, he lending me another.

Friday, September 16.—Took counsel with Captain Walmesley as to best way to get to Maritzburg, since I had to return to the Tugela for the baptism of the children. He advised *via* Greytown, and provided me with a *Kafir* guide on foot. Left early, got to Tugela by 8 a.m., crossed, and then to my disappointment found that the notice I had given overnight was insufficient to get the children together; so had to recross, promising to baptise them when we passed up to Kwamagwaza in the waggons.

The guide travelled so slowly owing to his carrying mealies for the horse—as we should pass no house by the way—that I off-saddled about twelve, and, pouring all the mealies on the ground, let the horse eat as many as he would, and then told the guide to get on quicker. But he was evidently knocking up; so there was nothing to be done, if I was to reach Mr. Udland's, a Norwegian station, but push on quickly alone. There was no road, a mere track, and not often this. However,

5. This has now been accomplished. St. Andrew's Station taken and entrenched by Lord Chelmsford is close to the Lower Tugela Drift, on the Zulu side.

I struck the waggon road after some hours. The country was exceedingly rough, and the road deeply cut in places. Doubting as to my way, I came, and was thankful to see it, to a little round mud house on a hill. Seeing pots and pans outside I knew it was a white man's. Tapping at the door, out came a man who spoke unmistakable American, and told me it was fourteen miles to the Norwegian's. So on again. The day, which had been overcast, now grew threatening, and rain began. to fall, while the hills were so covered with clouds that for hours I was scarce able to see my way.

However, on, on, till I was very glad to see a house. How little do people in England know what it is to see a house here over the wild, drear *veldt*, or on the lone mountain side! It was evidently a Mission station, and, as I thought, the Norwegian's. Upon arrival I found it was an American Mission station. The missionary, Mr. Abraham, was very kind, gave me refreshment, and offered me a bed; but wishing to get on to Mr. Udland's, six miles further, he lent me a horse and guide; mine was knocking up, and the guide miles behind; and so on again. Now the rain, which had been threatening all day, came down smartly, and the clouds made a dense fog all round, till by the time I reached Udland's it was getting dark, and I was soaked through.

Such a poor wretch I looked, draggled, way-worn, and dirty; the Kafir dragging my poor horse, utterly done up, through the driving rain. Udland gave me a change, wrapped me up in a wonderful great-coat, gave me some tea, and then to bed. He prophesied rain for the next three days, and said I must make up my mind to stay in the mountains with him that time. This made me anxious, as I wanted to get on to A., lest she should be ill or nervous about me. The old gentleman saw this, and said in very broken English, "Ah! well, I do like to see a man really married to his wife, and not only *involved*."

'*Saturday, September 15.*—Was thankful to wake and find it not raining, although the clouds were all down upon the mountains. Fancy three days in a little cottage amongst the hills, without a book, with an old gentleman who could speak but little English, and his wife none! So off again at 8 a.m. with *Kafir* guide. The old story again: horse knocked up, guide very soon *ditto*; got on a few miles, then track branched off, and had to wait till guide came up to learn the way. At last, as usual, getting weary of the pace, flogged the poor nag on till I got to a wretched house, where I found a sick German. Asked how far to Hermansburg. Six or seven miles. What could I do? Should I leave

30

the horse, which evidently could not go another mile, and press on on foot? Had the German a horse? Yes, but a "very wild one."

By this I thought he was unwilling to lend it to me. Would he show me the way to Hermansburg? He couldn't—he was sick. He then asked who I was. I told him, and then he seemed very willing to help me, gave me coffee, and said his boys were at school over the hill. Being Saturday it was a half-holiday, and they would be home in an hour if I would stay. One of them would ride and show me the way, and I could ride another of his horses, leaving my horse to be led on to Hermansburg when the guide arrived.

At last the boys came, the horses were saddled, when another difficulty arose. The mare I had to ride, the "very wild one," had a foal, and nothing would induce her to leave it, and, the foal not being able or willing to come, I had a battle to fight. As often as I turned her in the direction of Hermansburg, so often did she wheel round, and neigh, and shake her head, as much as to say, "You may try, but I have no intention whatever of leaving my foal." At last the lad took the rhim and led her, and, with a great shouting in the German tongue and flogging, off she went, and then she *did* go. A beautiful grassy plain all the way, and we *flew* it. Arrived, I saw Herr Holtz, the head missionary, and he promised to lend me a horse. But then he reported it to be still sixty miles (eight or nine hours' riding) to Maritzburg, and being nearly three o'clock I could not possibly reach it that night. So I resolved to stay, sending a letter by special messenger to say where I was.

Passed a very pleasant afternoon looking through this German Mission village. What excellent colonists these Germans make! how is it they have no colonies? Why do thousands go annually to America, and there become denationalised? Here was a model Christian settlement. All trades nearly are brought out from Germany to form these settlements; consequently you find a complete German village, and everything very trim. These Germans have dammed up a stream which runs through the settlement, and have made a really beautiful artificial lake in its midst. At one end of the lake is a water-mill for grinding corn, and they grind for this neighbourhood. This brings in alone an income of 300*l*. a year to the Mission.

Alas! we can make no such income, as we have no one to grind for in Zululand. Then there is a tanner, a bootmaker, stonemasons, carpenters, &c.; a flourishing German School; an upper school, also, for English boys, with two or three masters, one an Englishman. This is the central and largest German Mission station in South Africa; the centre of a system of missions sent out from Hermansburg in Hannover by the world-known Pastor Harms. It possesses the finest church I have yet seen in the colony—stone, and with a pretty spire. Here I met a Russian who knows England, knows Lowestoft, Norwich, Thetford, Bury, Diss, &c. So strange; the English master here has an uncle incumbent of Leiston in Suffolk.

Saturday, September 18.—Attended native service. About sixty Christians present. In middle of service three heathen natives came in—one a son of Song Panda, who was passing Hermansburg from Zululand. In the afternoon I took the English service, and preached to the seventy boys and a few English workmen on the station.

Monday, September 19.—Left Hermansburg early; road improved greatly, and country becoming much flatter. Called at New Hannover, a German Mission station, looked over church, and then rode on, and slept at Garbet's accommodation house.

Tuesday, September 20.—Rode into Maritzburg; a very dusty and hot day, having done about four hundred miles over a wild, mountainous, almost roadless and bridgeless country. A good breaking-in for African life, having only landed a week before beginning this journey. Everyone here wonders how I managed it—none more so than myself.

The next letter, which refers to the journal above given, was written from the Bishop of Maritzburg's house, where Mrs. Wilkinson had now removed from the Deanery.

Maritzburg. Oct. 16, 1870.
You will see by the above date that I am still here. I generally take a drive or a walk every day. In the morning we keep well to Zulu, working from 10 a.m. to 1.30 p.m. I think we are getting on, but every now and then we come to a standstill. We have no one who can teach us here. We have had such nice weather ever since we have been at Maritzburg. Yesterday was hot, but not hotter than an August day in England, and hot days generally end in a thunderstorm. We had a splendid one last night, and the air this morning is cool and refreshing.
I send you E.'s journal during his visit to Zululand. Our first object must be the church; after that we must think of our house. The present one must do for a while. Our sitting-room will be about twelve feet square, and our bedroom about twelve

feet by six. All the wood has to be brought from Durban to this place, which makes it so expensive. There is no wood about Kwamagwaza; at all events, none seasoned. We shall take up with us a great number of shrubs, fruit trees, &c. The oak grows so well here, but too hat to be of any use as timber; it grows as fast here as the lime-tree does at home.

E. has bought me such a nice horse; he says it is the very easiest he ever rode. I did fifty-six miles yesterday without being the least knocked up. E. got a nasty fall yesterday; he was riding with the Bishop of Maritzburg, and his horse put his foot into one of those numerous holes,[6] ten times worse than a rabbit-borrow, and E. made a somersault over its head. He is none the worse, I am thankful to say.

One more letter was written from Maritzburg, where a portion of the Mission party had been detained, by unavoidable circumstances, so late into the rainy season, that when those circumstances admitted of their making a move up country, they were unable to do so owing to the wet season having set in with unusual violence. The rivers were heavily swollen throughout the country, and travelling was rendered well-nigh impossible. One of the Maritzburg clergy in crossing the river Umbilo was swept away and drowned; and, other accidents of a similar kind having taken place, the party bound for Zululand were strongly advised not to venture upon their distant and difficult journey through a wild country, and at such a season, without roads and without bridges. It was felt, however, that the work in Zululand was suffering by delay, and a start was made under considerable difficulties not long after the following letter was written. The route out of Maritzburg lay up the 'town hill,' upon which many waggons had slipped and upset owing to the bad weather.

---

6. Made by the ant-eater, or ant-bear, as it is called in South Africa.

CHAPTER 3

The Start For Zululand, and First Impressions

Maritzburg. Nov. 16, 1870.

This will be, I hope, the last letter I shall write from this place, as we are looking forward, D.V., to make a start on Monday. We were to have started yesterday, but we had a letter from Mr. Robertson to say that he could not meet us at the Tugela till December 1.

I rode the other day to see some falls about seventy feet high. There had been a good deal of rain, and they were tumbling down magnificently; they are surrounded with pretty bush, so different to the usual country which is so bare of trees. One sees nothing but hill after hill covered with grass, and numbers of cattle grazing.

We have been so much struck with the good Church tone there is here amongst those who *are* Church people. The divisions here bring out the real feelings of people. There is a good choir—fourteen men, and ten or twelve boys. The men are all communicants; they are chiefly tradespeople. There are no really poor people, though they are very poor as regards money. I went the other day to see a woman, who I heard had come from Bedford, and I thought I could get some lace. Only fancy! she was ——'s servant for three years. She was enraptured at seeing me, and said, "To think that I should see my dear master's daughter and grand-daughter in Africa!" I went to see her chiefly because I thought she would like to see someone from her own county, and I was quite rewarded,

Poor E. is nearly worn out; this has been such a weary waiting for him, and now the oxen have not come; you know how anxious he is. When once we are off he will be all right, but no one at home has any idea what waggon travelling is. To get off at the time you intend you must tell the people you mean to start a week before you really intend doing so.

I meant to have written several letters this mail, but baby has taken up so much of my time, and one has to do of course a great deal that is done by servants at home, that the day is gone before you know it.

I cannot realise that next Sunday is Advent Sunday. It is so different to Advent weather at home—our midwinter is Natal midsummer. E. hopes to spend it in his diocese; it will be nice to begin the Christian year in it, for he has not yet officiated in Zululand.

This next letter was written in the waggon when out-spanned at the Umhlali, on the way to Zululand.

Umhlali. Dec. 1, 1870.

You will see by the above address that we are so for, thank God, safe and well on our journey. Although in the midst of the rainy season, we have not had a drop of rain, and of course we have been leading a picnic life. Baby has borne the journey wonderfully, and seems all the stronger for it. Fancy! every morning she is washed and dressed in the *open* air. We have a cow with us for her. This is a very hot day; we feel it all the more down on the coast, as we have been lately so completely amongst the mountains. The roads have been very good on the whole.

Last night E., Miss C, and I were lost. We went on riding in front of the waggons, and took the wrong track. We found out our mistake, and went back and found the right one. We followed it till we came to a river, which we could not make out how to cross; so we retraced our steps to a *Kafir* hut on the top of a hill, and there we saw the waggon-lights and fire down in the valley, but on the other side of the river. We roused up a *Kafir* and made him show us the way. He took us up the middle of the stream instead of across it, and we reached our temporary home a little before midnight. It was quite an exciting adventure; there was a good moon, and a beautifully soft air.

We are all of us, I think, the better for being so much in the air, and amongst the mountains. We sleep four in the waggon, and two underneath, and baby in her bassinet at the bottom of the cartel. E. sleeps in the tent. Will you tell —— that his tent is first-rate? Part of its belongings is a little camp set. I don't know what I should have done without it. It is most complete for two.

After a short stay with Captain and Mrs. Walmesley, the Zulu border agent, at his beautiful place upon the Nonoti River in Natal, the Mission party moved on to the Tugela River,[1] where a day was spent in unpacking the waggons; crossing the goods in a large punt; taking the waggons to pieces, and crossing them by the same means. Then the oxen had to be swum over, which is a long and troublesome matter, as they are driven with difficulty into the water, and have then to be kept swimming by men in the punt, who paddle across below them in the stream, cracking their long bamboo waggon-whips to urge the beasts across. When in midstream, a part, and sometimes the entire span, or spans, will turn back again. This loses a day, for they are too much exhausted to attempt the passage again the same day. Not unfrequently the weaker oxen are carried down towards the Tugela mouth, and drowned. The horses were tied on to the stem of the punt and towed across.

The labour involved in crossing our troops, material, stores, &c., in the late war, with the water in full flood, must have been enormous. The crossing of a single waggon and span of oxen at such times is exceedingly troublesome, and not unattended with danger; the greatest praise is due to those in command who effected the crossing of so much valuable life and property with little or no loss. From the Lower Tugela Drift the route to Kwamagwaza lies by Colonel Pearson's old position at Etyowe, as has already been stated.

Upon arrival at Kwamagwaza the following letter was written. Great as were the early discomforts to be met upon that first arrival, and for some long time afterwards, the same sunny, contented, uncomplaining tone which marked the whole life, marks this letter of 'first impressions.'

Kwamagwaza, Zululand at last. Dec. 12, 1870.
The mail (*Kafir* postman) leaves this tomorrow morning, so I must write you a few lines to tell you of our safe arrival here last Saturday, or rather I should say Sunday, morning, for it was 2 a.m. It was

---

1. This is the point at which all our troops and stores were crossed into Zululand. A pontoon bridge was, during the war, constructed at this drift.

full moon, and we trekked on late in order to arrive. Every one, of course, had gone to bed, having given us up.

And now for "first impressions." I am agreeably surprised. The scenery is much finer than I expected, and the house is much better, though our bedroom is only five feet wide, and about sixteen long; consequently we have to get into bed at the foot. When we are more settled I think we shall dine there, and take the dining-room for our bedroom. Our *drawing-room* is a nice room. We unpacked the piano this morning, and to our great delight it is in perfect order and perfect tune. We have a nice sofa, an oval table, a little work-table, and an open fireplace for burning wood. I am rather tired this evening, as we have been busy unpacking all day.

I have three handmaidens, but they require to be watched whilst they are doing their work; and as two cannot understand English, and I cannot talk much Zulu, we sometimes get into a muddle.

We were so highly favoured all through our journey, we did not have one drop of rain until we reached the Umhlali, where we slept the night at the house of the man who was driving us. The next night, and two following ones, we slept at Captain Walmesley's (a son of Sir Joshua), who lives close to the Tugela, and is the Zulu border magistrate. It rained heavily whilst we were with him. Then we had no more rain until we got to Mr. Samuelson's, one of our clergy, within twenty-five miles of this. We slept at his house, putting down our mattresses in his sitting-room. We had one most fearful storm, though, last week—thunder, hail, and wind; I never experienced such wind; we quite thought our heavy waggon would have been blown over. You can have no idea what it was, and the hailstones as large as hen's eggs. It lasted half-an-hour. We had just finished our dinner. You can imagine a little the force of the wind when I tell you that it drove, our heavy, big waggon quite twelve feet back.

We hope to begin our new church about March. The present one will not do at all. We have plenty to do, and our garden is in its own natural wild state. Our house, or rather I should say "Bishop's Hut," is on the edge of a steep hill, with another rising immediately in front. The garden, consequently, is on such a steep slope that we shall be obliged to terrace it. We stand

3,800 feet high, so you can fancy what a splendid view we have. As soon as the church is built we shall have a better house; but the church, of course, must be our first consideration. We have peaches, but it is too cold here for bananas. I am so sorry, for I have grown quite fond of them. As we came along we saw a good many bucks, and a kind of wild turkey.

The following letter, still fresh with "first impressions," will be read with interest. Indeed, all the letters from Kwamagwaza in Zululand must possess more than usual interest just now from the fact of their having been written front a point about midway between Colonel Pearson's position at Etyowe and Isandhlwana. On a clear day we could see the iron roof of Mr. Oftebrö's church at Etyowe, looking in the far distance across the Umhlatuzi valley like a sail at sea. On the other side we looked upon the Equdeni forest, from the neighbourhood of which that overwhelming mass of Zulus poured upon and destroyed our camp. Rorke's Drift was the post-office for Kwamagwaza, and the chief, Usihayo, was a near neighbour and frequent visitor, as was also Dabulamanzi, the great Zulu general, of whom we have all been reading so much during the Zulu war. I find two entries in my diary about these two Zulu worthies: '*Sunday, July 16,* 1871, Prince Dabulamanzi came. Promised to send his four sons here to be educated; had been talking of it with the Prince Cetiywato.' '*Saturday. September 7,* 1872, Usihayo came and dined with us.'

Kwamagwaza, Zululand. Christmas Eve, 1870.
This house is placed on the slope of a very steep hill, 80 that the garden has to be terraced down to a little stream in which are now flourishing arums and tree ferns. How I wish I could transport some of them to you at this minute when you are so busy decorating the church! Ferns of all varieties flourish and abound at the bottom of the garden. Opposite is another hill, not picturesque in appearance. To the right, on our side of the valley, are the Mission buildings, and to our left down the valley we get a peep of beautiful mountains. Though this is midsummer it is not hot; this morning, when we got up, it was bitterly cold.
This is our routine at present: Prayers in chapel at 6 a.m.; breakfast at 7 a.m.; then to wash, or bake, or iron, house work, &c.; dinner at 12; then Zulu for two or three hours; then a walk, or ride; tea at 7 p.m.; school at 7.30 p.m., ended by evening prayer;

bed at 9 p.m. Saturdays are half-holidays, so we are all going for a ride.

E. practised the other day upon a poor, wretched woman, and extracted one of her teeth—the largest, in fact, in her head. He *says* he drew it beautifully. He rushed in quite delighted for some water for her, and when he gave it to her she turned to her companion and said, "How kind these people are to us!"

We are gradually getting settled, but we have a lot still to unpack. We have three black girls, besides Tilly (an English servant girl); one is to be baptised tomorrow. One is to be married soon, and then I shall have a fresh one. The girls are a dreadful nuisance, so stupid and lazy, so inferior to the boys; but then, from time immemorial, they have been made the drudges, and looked down upon. We have to try and raise them out of this; but when they act as servants one is apt to forget what they are, and to expect more from them. But is not this provoking? You go into the kitchen and order a good fire for your ironing. You go in presently, the girls squatted on the floor, jabbering away, and your fire out! If you leave them a single minute they squat down and do nothing. But they are good-tempered, and mean to do right.

We have been here a fortnight today. We cannot realise that it is Christmas; in fact, it is better not to try. We are to keep it on Tuesday. The ox will be killed and cooked on Monday. All the Mission party sup with us on Tuesday. We shall be twelve, so Miss R. and I shall have our hands full preparing. A cheese we brought for the waggon journey will be considered a great delicacy. . . .

I left off here to go for a ride. The scenery about here is simply magnificent; such mountains! We saw a lovely view, a beautiful peaceful valley, with the Umhlatuzi running through it, and suddenly winding back again.

Christmas Day, 8 p.m.—All the others have gone to the Zulu service, and I am staying at home. This has been a most beautiful day, bright and sunny, but not too hot. I do not think that we can ever feel the heat oppressive here, as there is always a delicious breeze amongst the mountains. E. baptised eleven Zulus this morning; four big lads, three big girls, two small children, and two babies. We have now nearly one hundred Christians, men, women, and children; the work of ten years, but of course little was done the first five years. We had early celebration at 7 a.m.; then matins at 10 a.m.; the *Kafir* service at 11.30 a.m.

E. and I are going to ride to a place about ten miles off this week to meet the Prince Cetywayo,[2] and we shall take him some presents in the shape of a pair of guns which we bought him in Natal, and some smart table-covers which he will wear over his shoulders. They do not value anything shaped like a scarf; it must be seventy-two inches square. Money is of no use here, they will not take it; so if we want to buy a goat or a sheep we give them a blanket worth three shillings.

The king and the prince have both sent most friendly messages. The lieutenant-governor of Natal sent up messengers to the king to introduce E. to him, and they have been well received. You have no idea in what estimation the king and the prince hold themselves. They think they are the greatest people in the world, and certainly the king and prince have been, and are, great warriors.

It is sad to see how boys are kept from us by their parents or guardians. They keep them to herd their cattle, and the poor lads want to come so much. We saw this frequently on our way up. One nice boy, about fifteen, said, "I mean to come when I am a man," meaning when he was his own master, and I suppose that will be soon. The people think of nothing but of increasing their cattle.

There are always a number of heathen at the services on Sundays. One of our girls was baptised today, and one of them (Agnes) is supported by the Walsham Mission army. We used today the beautiful communion service given to E. by some of the clergy of Norfolk and Suffolk. We shall not begin the church for another year, for this reason: we can get the wood near here for nothing except the expense of carting and sawing out; but it must be seasoned a year. If we had it at once from Maritzburg it would cost us ten pounds per load. In the meantime we can make the bricks, lay the foundations, and build the walls next March; and then we can start the fresh station, for, of course, buildings will be wanted there. Whilst they are building

---

2. Cetywayo was always called 'the prince' in those days. His father, King Panda, brother of Chaka and Dingaan, was still living, but king only nominally; Cetywayo practically ruled the kingdom.

the house they will live in the tent we brought out. Six could sleep comfortably in it; it has two porches.

Poor E. is quite set fast with rheumatism. Our bed stands between the window—which does not fit—and the door, which leads into the open air. The other night it was very windy and cold, and we woke up thinking we must be out of doors, for the dust was blowing into my eyes. We must get a curtain up; but it is hard work to get behind our bed, as it takes up the space from wall to wall; consequently, when the bed is made, the mortar from the rough walls tumbles in, and when we go to bed we find it rather a gritty one. But we have not been here long, and when Edward and Ethel come I will make them comfortable. They ought not to come later than the beginning of August; that is full late; travelling in summer is very difficult. The best time for travelling is about June.

We eat porridge, and most delicious it is, made of mealy (Indian corn) meal, and taken with milk. We have given up eating sugar with it, as it takes such a quantity, and, of course, we have to husband our stores in this far country. We only use wine medicinally, or when we feel "done up."

This last letter ends the correspondence of the year 1870. It tells of the slow and troublesome ways of the Zulu girls. They *are* most trying; but there was no one upon the station—no one, indeed, elsewhere, of whom I ever heard, who could manage them as well as the writer of these letters. They delighted in her bright and sunny temper, and yet fully appreciated being kept in order by the firm and strict hand which was ever ready, if necessary, behind this genial disposition. A soft, weak character the Zulus utterly despise. A strong, strict, just, and genial one they respect and love. Refractory young Zulus, whom no one else upon the station could manage, were often brought to her, and subdued in the most remarkable manner;

I remember one in particular upon whom we had tried almost all the known remedies of the Mission station, and who was taken in hand at last by the subject of this memoir. The effect was most striking and enduring. We never afterwards had any trouble with him. When unmanageable I always said, 'Go to the *Inkosikazi* (chieftainess); she will settle the matter with you.' A young Zulu was once found secreted in the kitchen at night. Upon being told of it she went armed with a broomstick. Having poked and belaboured him out of his hiding place till he rose up and stood before her, a great, tall, strapping fellow, she gave him a terrible blowing up and then dismissed him, looking very sheepish and crestfallen. I never saw so complete a mastery of mind over matter.

Reference is made in this letter to the opposition on the part of parents and guardians in keeping their boys from the influence of the Christianity of the Mission station. The fountain head of this opposition was Cetywayo. Thousands there were in Zululand, compelled to fight against us during the late war, who but for his baneful heathen influence would years ago have embraced Christianity, and entered upon a civilised and useful life. Had liberty, on this point, been conceded by Cetywayo to his people, instead of keeping them up to the condition of a vast, man-slaying machine, as Sir Bartle Frere so well describes Cetywayo's army to be, the late war would never have come about. The first letter of the next year bears date:—

Kwamagwaza, Zululand. Jan. 12, 1871.
I have begun to write in good time this mail, and will try to write a little every two or three days, for unless I sit up at night I cannot write a long letter. I ought to be up at five in the morning, and go to church at 6 a.m.; but school is never over before 9 p.m., so that we cannot get to bed before ten. On Monday E. went to choose the site for a new station. He came back yesterday, and started today for Ulundi. There is to be a grand review; many thousands of Zulus will be present, and there will be a grand war-dance.[3] He will not be home for a week.

Now I must tell you that I have been to court. Cetywayo passed within ten miles of this, and expressed a wish to see E. But he was suffering severely, and unable to ride, so I went instead. Cetywayo was surrounded by his great men, and a younger brother had come to pay his respects, and had brought all his followers with him—several hundred. A war-dance was going on, and they sang their national song—really a grand thing. Cetywayo is a fine, tall, handsome man. None of the Zulus are as ugly as Frank (a Zambesi boy), and some of them are really handsome. They are fine, independent men, a great deal superior to the women.

The girls I have are the plague of my life, though they are very

3. It was estimated that at the *Umkosi*, or war-dance, this year, there were 30,000 warriors present. The Amahlabatini plain round old King Panda's *kraal* was black with the regiments as far as the eye could reach.

good girls on the whole; but if it were not for their own sakes I would not keep them an hour—I would have boys. Perhaps I am ironing a dress, for instance; I have left special injunctions to keep up a good fire. I go in—not a girl to be seen, and the fire all but out. You may always think of me on Tuesday and Wednesday mornings ironing.

Now we are beginning to get things comfortable. We have meat every day when we kill an ox. We salt a good deal, and then vary it with mutton. Mr. Glover shot me three pigeons this afternoon. Cape gooseberries are in great abundance, and peaches. Oranges will not grow here, only lemons. We have a quantity of a fruit called *grenadilla*.

It is pouring with rain, so there will be no school tonight, and I can go on writing—but my poor, dear E.! However, a Zulu hut is warm—warmer than a tent; but he has twelve miles to walk tomorrow, and he is still weak from his illness. The grass at the king's is poisonous for horses, so they could only ride half way. They were going in the waggons, but lung-sickness is amongst our cattle. We have lost about eight, and more are sickening. It was brought from the king's. Some of our people were plough-ing for him with our cattle, and they brought it back. Much better than if it had come through the white man.

It is astonishing how safe one feels here! We have no man in the house; we are three solitary females, and one sleeps in a detached house. Our doors are not locked, and yet I am not in the least degree nervous, although I always was a little at home when E. was out.

We are to have an ordination in Lent; Mr. Samuelson and Mr. Jackson for priests' orders, and a confirmation at Easter. Of course the only communicants here are those who came up, from Natal, with Mr. Robertson. We have celebration every Sunday at 7 a.m., Zulu service at 10 a.m., English service at 11.30 a.m., school at 3 p.m., and Zulu service at 7 p.m. E. preached his first sermon on Sunday. Of course Mr. Robertson helped him to put it into Zulu almost entirely, but Mr. R. was delighted. E. having such a good ear, and being naturally a good mimic, can read the language fairly well. But *talking* is the thing. When I begin, all my grammar flies out of my brain.

I went into Miss O.'s room just now, and found her sitting with two basins on the floor, which were rapidly filling with water.

We are quite watertight, but her rooms are not yet finished.

January 20, 8 p.m.—I have been cook during this week, and am surprised at myself. Today I produced a gooseberry-pudding—*such* crust, and all first-rate. The Cape gooseberries[4] are most delicious. I make jam of them, for we have hardly any batter, as all our cattle are ill with lung-sickness. Baby's milk is brought three miles, from a *kraal* where they are. free from disease, in order that she may have pure milk.

The worst of this place is that the soil is red clay, and in wet weather it is dreadfully muddy. We are free here from three things which they have badly in the colony: ticks, which eat your body; fish moths, which eat your clothes; and white ants, which eat your houses. E.'s horse is in a frightful state— covered with boils.

On reading this letter over I find that I have said a great deal about eating and drinking; but when we have to depend entirely upon ourselves for food, we find we get very like the Zulus, who, when they see a thing, ask if it is good to eat. Mr. Jackson brought E. a shrub yesterday, and said it bore a beautiful coloured berry. E. immediately said, "Will it make good jam?" and then burst out laughing at his question—so like the natives.

I am just beginning to play at the Zulu services. I find the pointing most difficult. We have a dreadful harmonium; we must pass it on to the new station when B.'s comes. The new station is to be called SS. Philip and James. Mr. Samuelson's is St. Paul's; this St. Mary's.

The ferns here are beautiful, and the tree-fern grows at the bottom of our garden. I wish you could have some of the beautiful flowers we have on the table, such as you see sheltered in greenhouses. I shall try and send some roots home, and also some birds. Mr. Glover shoots beauties, and is getting me some also. Where they are going (the new station) there are magnificent cranes. The breast of these birds would make a most exquisite muff—or rather two breasts—such long, grey, silky feathers!

January 28.—Since I wrote last we had a great fright. I think I have told you that we are constantly amongst the clouds. The other day Mr. Glover went out shooting; it was cloudy,. but it

---

4. A small round fruit like a large marble, enclosed in a husk, like a hop; the plant is of a low, herbaceous, creeping habit.

came on thicker, and, though not a mile from home, he lost his way. On the *veldt*, where there are endless Zulu paths, and not a tree as a landmark, it is difficult to find one's way in fine weather; but when the mist comes on, which it does most rapidly, you are hopelessly lost. We were in great anxiety in the evening, when he did not appear, and fired guns, &c. It was no use going to look for him, not even a Zulu can find his way about. We were still more anxious about him when morning came, and ten o'clock, and still he did not appear. So we sent about twenty men off. Shortly he made his appearance, having wandered to a *kraal* about twelve miles off. We were thankful enough to see him, and find that part of the night he had slept in a hut—he did not reach one till 1 a.m.—for it had been pouring all the night.

Another sad thing has happened—my poor, dear horse died yesterday. I had grown so fond of him, he was so sweet-tempered and quiet. I had a fall riding up here—my saddle turned round—and I hung on by the pommel. He stopped immediately, and was so quiet. It is very strange that one does not notice the "undress" of the *Kafirs*. I suppose it is their colour. The girls simply wear a string of beads until they marry.'

An account of the great war-dance—referred to in the foregoing letter—written upon the spot, by the compiler of this memoir, not by the author of these letters, will give an idea of what the strength of that army was with which we contended. How little did the writer think, when writing of these warriors and describing them '*formidable-looking fellows enough, and formidable, indeed, if they chose to be your enemies,*' that in so few years we should have them as our enemies face to face.

CHAPTER 4

Great Annual Review of the Zulu Army by Panda and Cetywayo

Kanodwenga[1] (the king's place). Jan. 14, 1871.
I must ask you to excuse a rough letter, as I am out upon a journey, and am writing this in a Zulu hut, squatting down amidst everything but what conduces to a decent, or even fairly legible, letter.

We started from home a week ago, and went a day and a half's journey to the north-west in order to explore a district in which we hope to plant our new station. We fixed upon what I trust will be a good spot. It lies amongst the hills, but is itself a comparative flat, upon a stream which has deposited so much of the *débris* from the hills above upon the valley through which it flows, that the soil seems abundantly rich. The grass in the neighbourhood is of the very best—a matter of great importance where so many cattle and sheep must be kept as is necessary for the support of a Mission station.

The cattle we saw in the district were the finest I have seen in Zululand, quite fit for exhibition, and some as large as buffaloes. The only drawback is the lack of wood; but this is in part supplied by an abundance of fine, stout reeds—more like canes—which are invaluable for thatching, shed-making, fencing, &c.; while for firewood recourse must be had, as in many parts of Thibet and China, to dried cow-dung, which burns like peat, and which, however much you may turn up your refined English noses at the idea, is by no means to be despised.

We have now got this new district formally granted to us by

1. Afterwards called by Cetywayo 'Ulundi.'

the king, and I hope that immediately after the Lent ordination, early in March if all be well, one of our deacons will be ordained priest, and sent with one of the young men I brought out with me, to begin the work. There are many native villages in this district, and several chiefs very friendly to us. We slept at the village of one of these chiefs,[2] and he treated us most hospitably. He kept patting me upon the back, and saying to Mr. Robertson, "So this is the Bishop, is it?" ("*Woza! um Bishopo, woza! hlala lapa eduze kwami.*") He must have me "come and sit near him."

Towards evening he left the hut, and, after a short absence, returned with another man, dragging something in the dusk behind him. Into the door, after a great struggle, he thrust a magnificent, cream-coloured goat, with horns thrown back over its shoulders. "I have brought this," he said, "to show the Bishop." It was a present to me for supper. In five minutes we heard the poor beast being killed outside, and in about half-an-hour had some of it smoking before us for supper. Before we left him next day we had service at the gate of the village. The whole place assembled; and again the chief insisted upon my being next to him, carefully removing every fly that settled upon me, as though I had been made of sugar.

We reached home again safely on the third day, and the next had to start again to come here, a two days' journey to the north-east. This is the king's place, and this is the great annual gathering of all the Zulu warriors throughout the kingdom of Zululand. The king had sent a special invitation to me to be present, that I might see the "strength of his country," as he expressed it.

The first day's journey across the mountains we accomplished on horseback, and then arrived at the head of the great valley which from time immemorial has been the home of the kings of Zululand. This valley is full of poisonous grass, into which it is impossible to take a horse. At the head of this valley, therefore, we left our horses, and sent them back, performing the rest of the journey on foot. We passed through a beautiful country full of flowers and flowering shrubs. There had been rain, and the whole air was scented like an English conservatory. The yellow

2. Umatyana, who narrowly escaped being captured by Lord Chelmsford's forces, a day or two before the Isandhlwana disaster.

and pink mimosa trees were in full bloom, jessamines of all kinds, fuchsia trees, orchids hanging down from the branches, gardenias, &c.

All the way as we came we passed groups of warriors trooping to the king's place, all dressed in their very best— spears, shields, plumes, tiger and leopard skins covering their bodies. Wherever the eye ranged across the hills it met companies of these warriors, all converging to one focus, the king's place. Out of bushes, from behind rocks, out of the gorges and beds of the rivers, they came and went singing their wild war-songs, and tramping as only these people can tramp; formidable-looking fellows enough, and formidable, indeed, if they chose to be your enemies.

About 3 p.m. we reached the top of a hill overlooking the valley in which the king's place is situated. In the centre of this valley lies the king's *kraal*, or town; all around for miles lie large military *kraals* or barracks, enormous circles of huts—I measured one which was 220 yards across. They are, upon ordinary occasions, merely garrisoned with a hundred soldiers or so, but now crammed to overflowing; indeed, temporary huts of green branches are being everywhere constructed to accommodate the host, which is supposed to number 30,000, and all these the very flower of the country, magnificent men, few under six feet in height, and very models in shape.

Upon our arrival we sent in messengers to report ourselves to *His Majesty*, In a few minutes a great man came out to us, bristling with tigers' claws, and told us that the king had placed two huts at our disposal close to his own. Here we rested for a while, and then a messenger came to say that the king wished to see us. We were marshalled with ceremony through a very closely-built stockade into an exceedingly clean courtyard, in which were several *beautifully*-built large, round huts, constructed with the precision and regularity of finely-made baskets. Here we were kept waiting a short while, as he was engaged with some-one upon business.

At last the master of ceremonies told us to come on. In we crept to the royal hut, and there, upon a pile of mats, and covered with blankets, lay the attenuated form of old Panda, who in his younger days had deluged this poor country with blood, and perhaps—with the exception of King Dahomey upon the west coast—had given, with his two brothers before him, the fatal orders for more cold-blooded massacres than any African king of whom the civilised world has heard. And now here he lay, an infirm old man of between seventy and eighty, and yet with an eye that scanned us like an eagle. He apologised for not shaking hands upon the plea of gout, and begged us to be seated. I gave him some rugs which I had brought out from England, with which he was greatly delighted. One especially pleased him. "That," he said, "I shall wear tomorrow at the great review."

We stayed with him for about half-an-hour, and then took our leave, and returned to our huts. Shortly after he sent us a bullock to live upon during our week's stay here, and a magnificent basket of native beer, milk, Indian corn, &c. The baskets are so beautifully made that they hold liquid.

We then visited the next greatest personage here, the king's favourite daughter, UBatonyile. Surrounded by a bevy of fair— or rather, I ought perhaps to say, particularly dusky females—sat the great princess—great every way. She is really a very interesting and intelligent person, about forty years of age, with a particularly pleasant expression. She is everywhere spoken of as a very good woman. She can read a little, and is at heart a Christian, though she dare not openly profess it. We had some very interesting conversation with her. She told us that she had her books with her; but she evidently keeps them out of sight of those about her, lest they should bring her into trouble. She said the Lord's Prayer to us (in Zulu, of course) without a mistake; and when we asked her if she used it every day, she said, "Yes; and not only that, but I am continually praying in my heart." I do hope that the time may soon come when she will be able to confess openly what she feels.

This morning the *crack* regiment, composed entirely of chiefs, and dressed far more magnificently than any of the rest, marched into camp. The Prince Cetywayo, the heir to the Zulu throne, is in this regiment. When it arrived, the king, wearing my beautiful rug, was wheeled out of his enclosure in a carriage into one of the great circles, which I have described, surrounded by military huts. Round him sat his great *ministers* and *courtiers*, ourselves amongst them. The regiment of chiefs formed in a semi-circle—the Prince Cetywayo in the centre—and went through all kinds of savage manoeuvres. The dresses of many of these chiefs Mr. Robertson estimates at 30*l.* value; at least, the magnificent feathers and ornaments would fetch this sum in Europe,

Altogether, it is a strange sight in a strange place. The continued roar and hum of voices throughout this vast camp of *savages*, which lasts late into the night as they sit round their watchfires singing their wild war-songs and relating the old traditions of their land—and then to feel that we are in the very midst (this is the centre) of Zululand, far removed from civilised governments, in the midst of these thousands of men, who might make mincemeat of us at small notice if they so pleased; and who, if we had ventured here forty years or so ago, would doubtless have done so, now most friendly to us, feeding us at their own expense, showing us every attention and kindness; and all this owing to the influence of missionaries scarce twenty years settled amongst them.

Slaughters such as once stained the old king's hands are now spoken of as things of the past— dark days of wickedness and cruelty which all believe can never come again. How different from the day when Captain Allen Gardner, the first missionary of Zululand, was driven from the country for telling of a faith which is now openly preached, and already believed in— secretly by some, without fear by others!

Yesterday a snake-charmer came into our hut to exhibit his power over one of the worst of African snakes, the deadly Imamba. He brought it out of a basket, and, just putting his great toe upon the tip of its tail, let it dart about towards us in all directions. What they do to these snakes to prevent being bitten by them is a problem. It is only the snake-charmer himself who is free from danger. I did not know this until the man had left the hut: but had it escaped the charmer's toe and bitten us, death would have ensued within twenty minutes—without remedies, that is to say.

I have some good remedies at home, and I shall never travel far without them, though in *our* part of Zululand, amongst the mountains, there are very few snakes. Here in the low, warm valleys they are numerous. One feels very thankful, in coming down on to the plains, that we have our home so high. Here it is intensely hot, enervating, headachy, fevery; with us it is rarely too hot, *sometimes* too cool, always breezy, at times a little too much amongst the clouds, for you must remember that we stand at Kwamagwaza as high above the sea level as the summit of Snowdon. Our height shows itself in father's aneroid barometer.

You know, perhaps, that a barometer falls as you ascend a mountain, the pressure being removed from the mercury in the mercurial reservoir. Well, when we unpacked it the needle pointed away down beyond "very stormy." At first glance we thought it was broken, until we remembered our altitude above the sea. It acts very well, quite as well as at home; only allowance must be made for our situation, and a new mean limit established to reckon by.

I went down to a stream[3] to bathe this morning. As I looked towards the Zulu camp, which was just out of sight above the hill, I could tell its exact position by the flock of eagles and vultures which hovered high in the air over the abundance of meat which is consumed upon these occasions. Writing of birds, I forgot to tell you that upon the site of our new station we saw two pairs of perhaps the most beautiful birds in Zululand. It is about the size of a crane, and like an enormous silver pheasant, with a splendid tail drooping almost to the ground. They live in the reed bed down by the stream. They are rare, and found only in certain districts.

The six poor pigeons I brought up from Maritzburg are gradually dropping off one by one a prey to the great buzzards, which abound, although we do all we can, by shooting, to get rid of them. I have only one now left. The other morning we picked one up still warm, but quite dead; it had just been struck in the back by a large buzzard, which had risen again, and hung high over its dead prey. They do not destroy the ducks we brought out from England, which seem to thrive well. Already we have young ones by them.

I forget if I told you in my letter of last month that the Lieut.-Governor of Natal sent a letter to the king by special messengers, introducing me to him. This introductory letter has been received with much attention by the authorities here, as they

---

3. Lord Chelmsford told me upon his return from the Zulu War that after the Battle of Ulundi the Zulu army passed over this stream and covered the whole range of hills beyond, till they were *black* with the flying hordes of warriors.

respect the English Government of Natal immensely.

We are now a little to the north of St. Lucia Bay, which a good map of Africa will give you, and about 650 miles or so from the Zambesi River. I never wish to go so far to the north as that. The diocese assigned to me by the South African Synod last year is bounded upon the north by the 26th parallel of S. lat., on the south by the colony of Natal, on the east by the Indian Ocean, and on the west by the Drakensberg range of mountains; and I have no intention of stepping, *episcopally*, beyond these boundaries. If we can manage, by God's help and blessing, to establish a chain of Mission stations at intervals of twenty miles along the highlands which extend northwards as far as 26° south, I shall be thankful indeed.

I am writing this upon my *bed*, the india-rubber air bed that Miss Mackenzie took up the Zambesi River. It is a capital thing to take upon a journey; it packs away into a space as small as that occupied by a waterproof coat, and is filled with air, pillow and all, by means of a small pair of bellows. Mr. Robertson sleeps on the other side of the hut, but upon a waterproof bed sent out to him by good Mr. Keble. We have much to thank him for; he helped this Mission much during his life. We have a waggon at Kwamagwaza which cost 100*l.*, his gift, amongst many other handsome ones, to the Zulu Mission. Did you ever hear that one of the last acts of his bounty was to give Bishop Gray, of Capetown, 1,000*l.* for South African Missions? Nobody knew of it; it was an anonymous gift, indeed I believe he always gave anonymously.

Second Sunday after Epiphany.—This is Sunday, and yet these poor, ignorant people are shouting, and rowing, and singing their war-songs, and carrying on their review, knowing not one day from another. In all this large multitude there are but ourselves, and the four Christian natives we brought with us as bearers, who are keeping the day as it ought to be kept. It makes one cast one's thoughts across the 7,000 miles which separate us from church bells, and quiet services, and happy Christian homes; so tenfold more dear because so entirely cut away from us. However, it is more profitable to look forward to the time when this land shall be full (as assuredly one day it will be) of Christian churches, and people living lives of industry and happiness.

I referred just now to the poisonous grass which exists in some of the valleys of this country. Here is an instance of its deadly nature. As we passed through the valley of the Umhlatuze on our way to Kwamagwaza, one of our horses put its head down once or twice only, and took a bite of grass. In three days from that time it was dead. It is a tall, soft, hairy grass. We return home next Thursday.

The next letter tells of the station life at Kwamagwaza. Mention is made of the time employed in the transmission of letters to and from Natal and Zululand. It was very tedious. At one time, when the Zulu country was much disturbed, and Cetywayo was supposed to be massing his warriors for an attack upon Natal—at which time no Natal *Kafir* dared enter the country—nearly five months passed without any communication with the outer world.

Kwamagwaza, Zululand. Feb, 20, 1871.

I am afraid our letters are very old as to date when you get them. We are better off in that respect, for yours are only two months old when we receive them. E. is very busy now working in his garden, for we received by our waggon the other day all the beautiful seeds sent us as a present by a London seedsman. It seems almost impossible to destroy life in a shrub here. Those we brought with us, and which we thought were quite dead, are now shooting out.

He is also very busy preparing examination papers for his two deacons, Mr. Samuelson and Mr. Jackson, who are to be ordained priests on Sunday week.

We have never yet experienced any great heat. Saturday was, I think, the hottest day we have had. The thermometer in the verandah, facing north—the hottest aspect—was 84°; but the next day at the same hour—12 o'clock —it was 62°: rather a change! and today it is lower still.

Our Zulu girls are improving immensely. One of them was married last Wednesday. E. married her to a young native who helps our carpenter. The service was word for word like our own, only in Zulu. Two of the young men—natives—had decorated the church so prettily with flowers. E. and I went to do something of the sort and found it done, and with flowers that you would prize in your greenhouse. Was it not nice of them? I

53

like some of the people here so much, especially the men who work for us. We have four men, and I have a boy. I quite forget they are black; they have such honest faces, and some are really handsome; of course they are Christians. There are seven heathen who work on the station.

I am going with E. and Mr. Robertson to start Mr. Jackson and Mr. Glover on their new station the week after next. We shall choose the exact spot for their house. We shall ride there—it is about twenty miles—take our blankets and sleep in a hut; one will be given up to us. I am quite looking forward to it.

It is very unfortunate having this lung-sickness just as we arrived here. We have lost a hundred and twenty cattle, and most of them cows. Of course we cannot send our oxen and waggon anywhere for fear of spreading the disease, and it is very expensive hiring waggons to bring our stores up all the way from Durban. We have just received two waggon loads; it costs about 8*l.* per waggon, and that added to the original price of the goods makes it come heavy. I am thankful to say that the disease is passing off; and shall we not enjoy butter when we get it again? we have not had it since Christmas. Some days we have no milk for coffee. All our cattle have been inoculated, so we shall never suffer like this again.

The weeks seem to fly by here, and yet we seem to have been here more than ten weeks. I suppose it is that we have done so much, and the days go quickly because they are so fully occupied. Do you know I am becoming a first-rate brewer! We have just finished ten gallons, and last week I brewed ten more; but it was rather hot work standing over a huge fire out of doors in a blazing sun.

You can imagine how we look for the mail, for we have only seen one passing Norwegian missionary since we have been here.

Poor Bishop Tozer has lost another of his clergy, I think E. will get to the Zambesi before he does. We are starting a new station in that direction thirty miles off, and another a hundred miles in that direction is in contemplation.

Tell S. I iron everything with flat irons, which I heat by putting them into a big pot and making a fire under. That is the way we bake our meat and bread, and boil our vegetables and puddings. Our Zulu girls are improving immensely.

These last words will be read with satisfaction. Under her firm and cheerful management the girls did improve most markedly. Almost all the girls who passed under her hands during our African life turned out thoroughly satisfactory; most faithful and good creatures they were to us in many a dark day of trouble and sickness, of which, as time went on, we had much. For eight months one of them nursed night and day with the tenderest care one of our children who nearly died during that period. Called up at all hours of the night to attend to the sick child's many little wants, I never heard one hasty or unkind word uttered by her.

In a waggon journey from Pretoria in the Transvaal to Durban, which extended from October 17 to Christmas Eve, this sick child was almost always either in her arms or in her charge, sometimes as much by night as by day; but, though naturally of a violent temper, she was gentleness and kindness itself to that poor little sufferer. 'I would go with her in the steamer,' she said, when we reached Durban on our way to England, 'but I am so afraid of the "*amanzi amakulu*" ("the great water"). I will be here, however, ready to take her when you come back again.'

St. Mary's, Zululand. First Sunday in Lent, 1871.
Since I last wrote E. has been down to St. Paul's station, about thirty miles from here. He went on the Saturday in order to administer Holy Communion, and he started off Mr. Samuelson's eldest son to the Cape College. The lad is about sixteen. His great wish is to be a missionary in this country, and of course he speaks like a native.

E. has been so busy working to get the garden into order, for it was merely a piece of land enclosed. The chief *weeds* in it were indigo and castor oil. He has planted a great many fruit trees, which I suppose will bear in seven or eight years. I have put in fifteen square yards of potatoes, and am now going to sow peas and beans. The cabbages we have would look fine at Covent Garden, and potatoes do well; in fact any English vegetables will grow. Tropical fruits we cannot grow.

The cattle disease is bad in many parts. The king says it is caused by witches, and in consequence is having people "smelt out" and killed, people who are perfectly innocent of course, but probably they have many cattle, and when they are killed the king takes the cattle.

One of Panda's queens came the other day with four princesses to be doctored; so we made them up a powder consisting of three grains of calomel, three of ginger, and ten of jalap. They came the next day to say that the powders had had no effect! so I am afraid we shall not gain repute for our doctoring. They had a horrid disease caused by the food they eat. The queen was *awfully* fat. She had bracelets above her ankles, but the fat hung down two inches thick over them; you never saw such a sight. Yesterday one of the princes came. We gave him some peach jam (which he liked immensely), some snuff, some sugar, and a fork. So you see we have plenty of *Royalty*, E. played to him on the piano, which, astonished him mightily.

Mr. Samuelson's daughter has been staying with us for the confirmation which took place this morning. It was such a charming sight. Three white girls; Miss Barker, Miss Samuelson, and our little nurse. Eight married native women, and twelve men. We had a procession. Hales headed it, carrying the beautiful banner; then the men and the women; after them the deacons, Mr. Jackson and Mr. Samuelson; then Mr. Robertson, then Mr. Glover, carrying the pastoral staff, and lastly the bishop. They sang the 24th Psalm. I took it up with the congregation as they entered. The service of course was Zulu, and E. gave them an address in Zulu. He has a very nice chair which he had made in Durban.

Mr. Robertson presented the candidates singly. Then we had a recessional hymn. No procession could have been in better order, and they sang remarkably well. You must remember that they had never done or seen such a thing before. I am organist now. My greatest difficulty is that when I look at the music, in either hymn or canticle, I often lose my place, and the maze of Zulu words is most perplexing. Then, again, I find I play too fast, and E. and Mr. Robertson are (like Dean —— in the *Lord's Prayer*) obliged to skip long words.

On Sunday next, Mr. Jackson and Mr. Samuelson are to be ordained priests. The Tuesday after Mr. Jackson and Mr. Glover start for their new home. Mr. Robertson, E., and I accompany them to choose the site for the new house, &c. We shall be away for about three days, and we shall live in a hut. During this rainy weather it is better than the tent, because if the ground is wet it streams inside the tent. We shall live principally upon *Kafir* food.

The natives are such pleasant people, they always have a smile and a greeting for us. The men were rather astonished when I superintended their work in the garden and showed them practically how to do some things, and said I ought to have been a man.

Fire is a fearful thing here, the one calamity of which we have a great dread; I pray we may be preserved. It is dreadful to be burnt out of house and home in England, where you are surrounded by kind friends and *shops*, but here you can have no idea what it would be. It is a custom of the natives to burn the grass when it gets long in order that they may have fresh green grass for their cattle. It is beautifully green three weeks after it is burnt. One of these numerous fires might come to us. Our precaution is this: when the wind sets *from* us we burn all round the premises, for fire will not cross either a burnt patch or green grass. We have sent for a peck of acorns, and we are going to plant an avenue.

I would write longer letters, but you have no idea how busy I am, and when I come in from school every evening at 9 p.m. I am too tired to sit down and write. I am either cooking, or ironing, or mending in the morning; in the afternoon we have school, then I garden or walk, for it would not do to take no outdoor exercise; and then the day is gone.

I wonder if you would think our house very rough, if you were to come straight to it from the ship. What do you think the floors are covered with? A substance brought from the cattle *kraal!* When I first heard of it I was horrified, and declared I never would have any room of mine "smeared," as they call it. The floors of all our rooms are cemented, but the verandah is brick, and very soft. I was obliged to come to it at last. The way they do it is this: the girls bring the *substance* and "flop" it down; then they pour some water on it, and go down on their knees, and spread it all over with their hands. Then the smell whilst it is being done! Ugh!

They use this *substance* for almost everything. They cover the walls inside and out with it; use it like mortar; and where Mr. Jackson and Mr. Glover are going it will be their only fuel. When used for this last purpose it is placed in the sun to dry, and then piled away like peat. E. says he can fancy B., when reading this, bursting out laughing and saying, "What disgusting people! only fancy E. taking that beautiful creature to live amongst such nasty ways!"

No one was more decided than I was in saying that it should not be done; but we cannot afford wooden floors, and it is very difficult to get up cement. We brought four casks from Maritzburg; but it was so heavy that going up a mountain the waggon stuck, and we were obliged to take it out and leave it there, miles and miles away from a white man's house, covered with a tarpaulin. It has since been got down to the Tugela, and there it lies. So what must we do but *smear?* When it is dry, which is in about one and a half hour, it is really clean and smooth.

Our drawing-room has three doors in it, one opening into the open air. The dining-room has four doors, two opening out of doors. So does E.'s dressing-room, which is his study also. Our kitchen lies just behind our house. E. and I have been intending for some days to make a sketch, but it has been so wet. Today, however, it is lovely; but he is busy examining Mr. Jackson, so I do not know whether I shall get him. I am writing in E.'s study, looking out on to beautiful hills.[3] On a hill close by we can see the sea on a clear day; but I have not been up yet, though it stands very little higher than we do.

This is not like Lent to us; indeed none of the seasons can we realise. I think at home the dull weather of Lent makes us welcome Easter more. We decorated the church yesterday with a white flower, very like orange blossom, and with the most beautiful pink lilies, such as you would see in greenhouses.

Tell Mr. Prestwich[4] I should like him to come and hammer about us here. We have gold I am sure; there is plenty of quartz. I often find myself looking for a diamond, and we ought to have coal. Some of our party have been to a forest a day's walk from here. Mr. Glover shot some beautiful birds, and saw lots of monkeys with the long black hair which is used for muffs. Leopards, panthers, and buffaloes are there also. He heard the former in the evening near their hut.

You ask about beef and mutton. The former is sometimes very good. The worst of it is it will keep fresh only two days; we

---

3. These hills were towards Rorke's Drift. One would possibly be Isandhlana, or hills very near it.

4. Later Sir Joseph Prestwich, the geologist.

have, therefore, to eat so much at once, and salt the rest. It is no joke salting a quarter of an ox; rubbing and turning is hard work. The mutton is not very good.

For the benefit of African travellers and missionaries here is my receipt for brewing. I make ten gallons at a time. Nine pounds of sugar, one pound of hops, a cupful of camomile flowers, two soup platefuls of mealies (Indian corn). I boil all this for about one hour and a half, then put it into the cask. In the morning I add a quart of yeast. My yeast is very good. Try it one day. Of the old baking save a piece of dough; the night before you bake take the old dough and mix it well with six table-spoons of flour and two of sugar; mix it with lukewarm water. It must neither be too stiff nor too thin. Do try this; our bread is capital.

CHAPTER 5

Cetywayo's Way of Governing His Country; An Insight to His 'Reign of Terror'

Reference is made in the letter which concludes the last chapter to the custom existing in Zululand of 'smelling out' people supposed to have been guilty of witchcraft and destroying them, their cattle becoming the king's property. This was the case to a terrible extent during the prevalence of the lung-sickness amongst the cattle in Zululand.

There lived near our station a very good heathen family whose hearts were with us; they were constantly at church on Sundays, and frequently in our station on week days amongst us, or our native Christians. There were several fine, handsome young fellows in this family; one, a great friend of ours, some six feet two inches in height, a good shot who often went out hunting for us. It came to the ears of their chief that they were Christians at heart, and intended coming over to us. This made their chief jealous. He was a bad man, and immediately set on foot a witchdoctor to smell them out, and accuse them of having caused lung-sickness amongst his cattle.

This is never a difficult matter where a chief has large bribes to offer the witchdoctor. The incantations went forward, and this family was taken as having bewitched the cattle. It was reported to Cetywayo, who ordered the destruction of the family. Our young hunter came to me and told me what was about to happen—that an '*impi*' (a band of spearmen) had been sent out from the king to destroy his family. I told him to watch keenly for tidings of their approach, and apprise his family in time to escape. I gave him a long, thick serge shirt to watch in, for he had to sit about upon the hills all night, as it is in the early morning that the Zulus make their attack upon any devoted village. The captain of the 'impi' tells off his men, and each man stands by the little hole which forms the entrance of the hut, spear in hand. As the inhabitants come creeping out down goes the spear into them, as a seal hunter standing over the seal holes of the Polar seas plunges his spear into the seal as it comes up to blow. Notice was given in time to the family in question, and they fled, taking refuge in the surrounding villages, and hiding there.

This was reported to Cetywayo, and he issued fresh orders to the effect that any village found harbouring any member of this family should also be destroyed. For several days the work of destruction went on, and, as is usual in such cases, those who escaped with their lives, or wounded, having lost relations and perhaps their all in this world, fled to us and sought the protection of the English upon the Mission station. We are able to show kindness to these poor people when in such sore distresses, and we not infrequently find that they have no wish to return after a while to their old heathen life, but ask to be allowed to stay on the station and be prepared for baptism.

On this particular occasion I had to go out to the 'impi' early one morning as they came up from a stream below a *kraal*, to separate, and to liberate some of our Christians' cattle from those confiscated. They had been washing the blood from their spears. Such a sight I never saw before, and never wish to see again. They looked like an army of devils. I should have known some of them at any other time, but now they had worked themselves up into such a state of frenzy, to do those deeds of blood, that the form of their countenances was altogether changed. Fathers are sent to kill sons, sons their fathers, brothers their brothers and sisters, and so forth, for, says Cetywayo, 'it makes the heart of my people stout for the day of battle.' These slaughters, terrible as they are, not unfrequently turn to the Church's profit. The Mission stations gain new converts, and so *the fierceness of man turns to God's praise.*

Kwamagwaza, Zululand. March 23, 1871.
I have been from home with E., and I must give you a little account of our journey. We left home on Monday about 9.30 a.m. It was a very hot day; but we had, as we generally have, a delicious breeze. I had not gone a mile when my horse went into a hole and came on his head. I, of course, came off, and he fell on to

the top of me. However, I am most thankful I was not hurt or shaken in the least. We rode on till about 2 p.m., when we off-saddled by the side of the beautiful river Umhlatuze, and we all ate our lunch and *drank of the river*. We stayed for an hour, and then rode on. We found our friends about 6 p.m.; they had only just arrived, although they had started on the Thursday before, having to go round hills by the waggon. I was very stiff and sore when I arrived, but we found a good supper, Mr. Robertson having killed an ox, and with nice hot coffee we had abundance. E. and I slept in the waggon.

The next two days we explored the country to find the best spot for the station. It had to combine several things. In the first place water, and that near at hand; stone; absence of *Kafir* gardens; and earth for making bricks. At last we found a spot where all these requirements were to be had. On the Thursday we left our friends, and rode for another day to the grand forest, from which we get all our rough wood—a most magnificent place, with such trees! Oh that we had a sawyer here! Each tree would have its own sawpit, as it could not be moved from where it fell.

At night we slept in a *Kafir* hut (the first time I had done so). It would have been pleasant enough but for the cockroaches. If there was one there were a thousand. When all was quiet we could hear them rattling about, and occasionally they dropped from the roof into my ear. We also had a rat amongst the *Kafir* pots. We stayed at this place two nights. It was time, too, we should leave; my breakfast the morning I left being a cup of coffee, about two inches of buck, and a few roasted mealies.

I think I should admire this country more if there were trees; but with the exception of this place, and a few others, you do not see a tree for miles—merely bare hills one after the other, and all exactly alike. The long way the waggon has to come makes us feel far away from every one, but really we are not so far. I could ride to Durban in four days; that is at the rate of thirty miles a day, and I did that last week, and over a country with no English roads, but sometimes hanging on to the horse's mane up steep places, and having to go down the same. I said to E. the other day, "I would rather ride up the back stairs at W. than up this place." But one great advantage is that the horses are bred in the country and therefore accustomed to it. Few

English horses could do it.

I have used the gun J. Sawbridge gave us. It is such a nice one, and so light that I can shoot with it easily. A hawk was carrying off our chickens one day. We found our friend sitting on the top of a tree close by. So E. took the gun and let me shoot, and I killed him. It was what P. would call a "right-up" shot, breast on. E. skinned it; it has a beautiful plumage.

Indian corn is very plentiful in Natal this year. It is only two shillings per sack. This time last year it was twenty-five; but we have not much, there has been so much wet. The men were all so busy getting our house ready, they were not hoed at the proper time. Tobacco grows very well here; all the people are inveterate smokers and snuff-takers. For snuff they grind the leaves on a stone. They grind all their corn also on a stone.

Our latest news came *via* Mauritius, and arrived before the mail which brought us tidings of the fall of Paris.

The mention here made of shooting the hawk gives occasion for stating that Mrs. Wilkinson was one of those people who seem born to do everything. These varied and special gifts were most valuable to one living a rough life in a far land. Her hand was very steady, and her aim most accurate. I remember upon one occasion when we were staying at the Amaswazi Mission station of Derby, New Scotland—occupied in the late war by part of Colonel Wood's column—a young Englishman was practising with his rifle at a bottle, set at a long range, upon a cairn of stones. Though a particularly good shot he missed the bottle several times. 'Give the rifle to me,' she said, 'and let me try.' At the first shot down went the bottle.

The fall from her horse related in this letter was not owing to defective horsemanship. The horse, while cantering, put its foot into an ant-eater's hole, and came down upon its head. Mrs. Wilkinson was an excellent rider and managed horses perfectly. We rode, during our African life, many thousands of miles together. Her horseback journeys were recorded in South African newspapers. She was the envy of Dutch wives and daughters in her powers of endurance. Colonial-born women and girls looked upon her as a wonder. She was frequently on ahead of the rest of the party, and into the halting-*kraal* for the night before the rest were in sight. She was independent of all assistance, would mount, and off-saddle, and knee-halter her horse as quickly and better than many of us.

St. Mary's, Zululand. March 31, 1871.

The three boys, Hali, Charlie, and Billy, together with Charlie Gower, one of Bishop Mackenzie's Zambesi boys, have come up from the Cape. E. has his hands full now. He teaches them from two to five. Charlie and Billy can play very nicely on the harmonium, and Charlie can sing very well in parts. I shall have to keep up their music; but I must teach them afresh, for they cannot play from notes. They have been taught either by figures or letters, but I do not know the system. I have plenty of playing now on Sundays—at our early celebration, our English service, and the full Zulu service—so that by one o'clock I am rather hoarse, and then again evening service. They sing so exceedingly slow, but I must gradually quicken them. These Cape boys sing very quickly.

Such a kind letter came from the Bishop of Grahamstown, who had heard E. was not well, and begging him to go to Grahamstown for change of air, as that place is bracing. People think that because we are nearer the line we must be hotter. There was never a greater mistake, for there are some mountains exactly under the line that are rarely without snow. The poor boys from the Cape have been shivering this morning, though just like an April morning in England—bright and sunny, only without the cold east wind. The air is very fine; it is like drinking champagne—you would delight in it. We get rather too much wind to please us, as it comes rushing up the side of the hill from the valley. The verandahs are a great comfort; they keep the house so deliciously cool, and we generally sit in them.'

Referring to the subject of temperature touched upon in this letter, it should be remembered that altitude within and just outside the tropics, rules the temperature, and not latitude. When upon one occasion I was in the North Transvaal, and within a day's ride of the tropical line, a little girl, the daughter of the settler with whom I was staying, brought me an icicle as long as my arm, which she had broken from the eaves of the house.

St. Mary's, Zululand. April 27, 1871.

The women bring their babies to me, I suppose because I have a baby. I doctor them homoeopathically, as I know I cannot do them much harm that way, and it may do good. We have got quite a nice flower-garden now. The other day E. sent Mrs.

Robertson a bouquet of geranium, roses, double petunia, heliotrope, mignonette, verbena, and a beautiful, wax-like flower that grows in a greenhouse at home. We have also beautiful portulacca and blue hydrangeas. Our flower-garden is upon a terrace. Stones form the edging, as we have neither turf nor gravel. We have put good black earth into the beds; the ground around is red clay, so that it does not look so bad as you may imagine.

May 2.—Your letter just received, in which you tell of having heard of our arrival at Kwamagwaza. The picture of the waggon crossing the river in the "Net" is a very faithful one; we did not cross the Tugela, however, in the waggon, but by boat. The river was seventeen feet deep, and such a rushing, swollen stream it was! I thought they would never have dragged the poor horses across, for, owing to the strong current, we were carried in the boat far down. When not swollen, the Tugela is easy to cross, for the banks are flat, and level with the water. It is when you have to go down a bank as steep as the top of the garden at Felmersham and huge boulders of stone in the bed of the river, that it is very disagreeable.

Not only does it look very horrid to go down, but the bumping over the stones sends you from one side of the waggon to the other. We were always two in the waggon at such times, for the one who held Edie could do nothing to help herself, so in bad places the second person helped to steady the nurse. Edie used to scream as soon as the waggon stopped, while the more it jolted the better she slept. We never journeyed more than four hours, so that we could feed her well.

A vulture settled yesterday on a tree in our garden, and I rushed in and loaded the gun, but before I got out again the wretched thing had flown.

You ask about domestics; they certainly are a trial. The girls would ruin any one's temper; they are always running away just at the most critical state of the fire, which, being of wood, constantly wants making up.

This will make you laugh. E. asked the other day at dinner for a fork, and one of the girls handed it to him, not by the handle, but by the tip, to which he decidedly objected. Again, our door had been freshly painted, and we discovered on it a distinct heel-mark and five toes. This was Miss Agnes again! She is a funny girl. We have a nice terra cotta water-bottle, which to us, up here, is priceless. She had orders never to take it from the house to fill for fear it should be broken. Fancy my horror the other day when I saw her returning from the water-barrel with the precious water-bottle on her head! She is very fond of performing on the dustpan like a tambourine.

I am sorry to say that the piano is in a most frightful state of discord. The damp here in the summer is more than you can imagine. A book will be perfectly mouldy in a day. As soon as the dry season has fairly set in, E. is going to try and tune it. A great chief[1] came here the other day, and he was charmed when I played the Russian National Anthem. He did look so ridiculous. He had on a large, American planter's hat, and a short, white coat, under which his tails appeared, acting as a bustle.

The only clothing the men wear are tails in front and behind; they are narrow strips of the fur of some animal. But we are so accustomed to see them that we do not think anything of it. In the colony they are obliged to wear a blanket or shirt.

We shall soon be looking very ugly here, for when the grass gets old and long they burn it all off, and in about a fortnight the fresh, young grass springs up. E. has been so busy lately that he has not had time to make another sketch of this place. Every afternoon from two to five he has the four Cape boys at lessons, and he has still a great deal of writing.

The young grass only springs up quickly again after the burning of the grass if burnt towards the *end* of winter, when the first showers of spring begin to fall. If the old grass be burnt early in winter, the *veldt* so. burnt remains black and dusty till spring. Hence the danger to our forces during the Zulu war of the grass being burnt in May. It will not spring again until September.

St. Mary's, Zululand. May 16, 1871

We can buy young cattle, a year old, for 1*l*. In two years' time, after we have broken them in, they are worth 4*l*. They do not cost us anything to keep, for we must have a herd-boy for our cows, and he can herd 200 as well as 100. We have now only about 100 head; 130 to 140 have died; and now we have only two cows in milk. The Zulus are so stupid; they bring up the calves with the mother, and the cow will not give her milk

---

1. This was Usihayo, with whom the Zulu war began.

unless the calf has previously fed, and is by her side. The consequence is that, when a calf dies, the cow is no longer milked. Sometimes, however, they stuff the skin of the calf with grass, and lay it down in front of the cow, and then she thinks it is her calf, and she gives her milk.

So poor Mrs. Gray is dead; what a dreadful loss she will be to the bishop, and also the whole of the province of South Africa! We can hardly believe that the strong, hale-looking woman should be taken, and the poor bishop left, who looked so worn out, and so much more frail, when they were with us.

Our new station is going on famously, and Mr. Jackson is charmed with the place. It is much superior to this place. We are going to begin tomorrow to make 150,000 bricks. Mr. Robertson says we can make 2,000 in a day. As soon as these are made, E. and Mr. Robertson are going to the extreme end of the diocese, as marked out by the South African Church, *viz*. lat. 26°, close to the Drakensberg. We have been offered a tract of land up there, and we have a missionary ready to go; so E. and Mr. Robertson are going to inspect. They will have to walk; just about the time you get this he will be setting off. Pray for him that he may be preserved in all dangers, and may be brought back in safety, having successfully accomplished his work.

You would have been so horrified if you had been here the other day. We were out of mealies; so Mr. Robertson, when he was down at the Tugela, bought some for us. Well, they were brought to me, and I put them away in the store room. The next morning I went in with our man who was going to rub over the bacon for me, and I exclaimed, "Martyn, what a dreadful smell! Is the meat bad?" I smelt everything in the place, but could find nothing wrong until I began to give out the mealies to grind for porridge, and it was *them*. They had been kept in a hole in the cattle *kraal* for a year, and you can imagine the kind of smell there was. "Oh!" said Martyn, "the Zulus like the mealies better when they smell like that." But we could not eat our porridge.

Last Sunday E. spoke to four of the most promising of the young men here about being ordained to the diaconate. They are to think of it for a month; and at the end of that time, if they are willing, they are to form a class for extra instruction. Two are Hottentots, one is a half-caste—his father being an Englishman, his mother a Zulu—the fourth is a pure Zulu. E. would send them about fifteen or twenty miles away from a station over which a white clergyman presided, by two and two, so that they could be overlooked and helped in any difficulty. They would employ heathen boys as cowherds, and heathen girls to help their wives in their houses, and in time they would form a little Christian community, besides their influence on all around them. Two of our Christian boys, lately baptised, worked for Martyn—one of these Hottentots—and under his influence, and that of his good wife, they became Christians.

Did I tell you that we can see the sea so plainly (over Etyowe) from our garden, or rather just at the back of the garden? It is about fifty miles off. The school building gets on nicely. Three outside walls are finished, but the inside walls have to be built. Little Putu is called by the natives "Unohleka," *i.e.* "one who laughs." She sits up so prettily in her nursery and receives her Zulu visitors who come to *pay their respects.* Our good Christians are our best missionaries. They all employ some heathen lads and girls. The lads work on their little plots of land, or herd their cattle; the girls help in the house as nurses, &c. The influence of a good Christian household on such lads and girls is very remarkable. They are the nurseries of our native Church; whereas the careless and unsatisfactory Christians, instead of helping us in our work are hinderers of it.

Last Saturday we all bumped down in the waggon to Mr. Samuelson's station, about thirty miles from here. Martyn drove us: we had four other boys with us; Telesa, our own dear, good, faithful girl; Ucwangube (there is a "c" click in this name), our new girl, and Adele. We took down a sheep for them all, and plenty of meal, so we did not eat up poor Mr. S. We started at 8.45 a.m., outspanned at 1.30 p.m., cooked our coffee and porridge, ate our bread and brawn, inspanned at 4 p.m., and arrived by moonlight at 7 p.m. I do believe the moon is much brighter here than in England; of course the atmosphere is much clearer; we can see to read the smallest print by moonlight. We can also see the stars in the horizon, which we never can in England. Then again, seeing the sea fifty miles off shows what the atmosphere is. It is a wonderful air up here; we hardly ever hear of consumption, although often of asthma.

Last week we had a very nice ride. A little child had been

brought to us with a broken arm, and we rode to see it over such a pretty country which we had never seen before, and over flats splendid for a gallop. It was about ten miles off; however, just as we got to the *kraal*, E.'s horse turned lame, and the child we found was two miles farther on, so he took mine and went on.

My horse has a trick of rearing when he is girthed up if he has not got his greedy old nose in a basket of mealies. The little mare has never got over the last day's ride home from Amaswaziland. It was so frightfully steep and stony, and she wore her hoof down to the frog. I walked back with her till I came to the river, and then I had to jump up and rode over. When the others caught me up we nearly lost ourselves amongst some marshes and dykes which the horses did not like to jump. Miss R. looks at me with envy when I jump up on horseback without any help.

One of our boys has just come to us with such a terrible finger. He quarrelled with a Zulu about a stick, and received a blow which cut open his finger and smashed the knuckle-bone, and there was the end of the bone sticking out. We could do nothing but bandage it up with arnica and water. The poor boy is in dreadful pain, and is lying in our dining-room groaning. I have just given him some henbane, and am going to follow it up with a dose of salts. Their sticks are awful things, having huge heads, and make dreadful wounds.

Little Edith gets on famously with her talking, but alas! very few English words. She was singing a Dutch song the other day. Then, again, she will talk Norsk, which she picks up from the Norwegian children on the station. But Zulu she always speaks, and the English words she does say are Zuluised. Her *r*'s are *l*'s. Yesterday another girl came to us, and I quite hope we shall be able to keep her, for her owners are dead. A boy also joined us as we came home from Mr. Samuelson's, and said he wished "*ukufunda*," "to learn."

A little time back Cetywayo gave E. such a lovely ox. We put it into the waggon the other day, and broke it in as we went down to Mr. Samuelson's, and it behaved beautifully, and pulled, Martyn said, like an old ox. I bought a splendid bull the other day for fifteen shillings (5 lbs. beads). Very soon after a white man offered me three pounds for it, but I would not take it; I want it for the waggon. Any day in the colony I could get 5*l*. 10*s*, for it. There is a great trade going on in guns, the Zulus want them so much. They will give you five oxen for a gun which costs 3*l*. 10*s*. Each of these oxen is worth 6*l*. There is profit, if you like! But then the trade is illegal. I do not know why Government maintains the law, for they must know how it is broken.

Then, again, we must not sell powder or caps; the latter the Zulus are mad after. I heard of a man who got a good cow for fifty caps, which are worth sixpence, a cow being worth three pounds. The only thing we ever buy with powder and caps is game. The other day we bought a buck for three caps and three charges of powder. Lead or shot we may sell. The gun and ammunition trade has lately begun amongst the Zulus, which has now ended in almost every warrior possessing a gun, the chiefs possessing many.

In that day there were but few guns in the country. We gave Cetywayo the first pair of good guns he ever possessed, and for this we had to obtain an order from Mr. Keate, the Governor of Natal. When application for the order was made to him he said, 'For my part I do not see why we should object to the Zulus possessing guns; the *assegai* is a much more fatal weapon in their hands.' That, however, was nearly ten years ago, but it is still true. In our recent engagements with the Zulus they fired comparatively little, and with little effect. Their most deadly work was done with the *assegai*—a weapon with which they are familiar from their earliest youth.

In 1870 a good gun was not known in Zululand from a bad one. We were calling one day upon Mahanana, one of Cetywayo's brothers. A trader had passed his *kraal* just before us, and had bartered two guns for three oxen. Mahanana brought them out, and said, 'Here they are; what do you think of them? Let us try them.' Seeing at a glance that they were gas-piping fitted into deal stocks and stained red, we said, ' No, thank you; if you like to go to yonder tree and try them, we will stay here and tell you what we think of them; but we advise you not to attempt to fire them, as they will probably burst.'

What can these Zulus think of English traders, calling themselves Christians, who take such advantage of the ignorance of these poor fellows! It has been said lately that Portugal has promised to co-operate with us in stopping the gun trade upon its coasts, especially at Delagoa Bay. What can Portugal do, however, with its miserable little penal settlement of Lorenzo Marquez—a mere handful of mud hovels—as the only representative of its power on that part of the coast? So little was it possible to guard even the Natal frontier from this illicit trade, in the years preceding the Zulu war, that when we were in Zululand cases were smuggled over the Tugela from Natal into Zululand, with our name and Mission painted upon them, filled with guns and ammunition for the Zulus!

St. Mary's, Zululand. May 23, 1871.

We had such a treat yesterday. The waggons came, and with them the precious box. It was such a treat unpacking and handling the things you and M. had sent. At the bottom of the box were four volumes of the *Monthly Packet* beginning with the largest series, and Miss Yonge's *Caged Lion*. It was only two nights before that I had said how I should like a nice story book. Everyone at the station also is eager to devour the fresh books.

And now to business. From Bebington we received tunics, frocks, skirts, and one dress, which are all pretty; especially useful are the striped shirts—they are what we want most—and white trousers and coats. When a native goes down to the colony he is always charged with commissions from the others, and the Sunday after his return they look so neat and nice. One man looked so well last Sunday; he had on a grey flannel shirt, a pair of white corded trousers, and a very light cloth coat. He looked quite handsome. Mrs. C. J. sent a very useful bundle, also Miss M. The knickerbocker suits are specially good. North Peckenham working party sent a most excellent bundle; handkerchief are always useful, I cannot have too many, but the material may be of the commonest. The flannel and calico, twelve yards of each, will be most useful, the poor things feel the cold so much.

From Faringdon and Exeter we received such a capital bundle. From Derby also we had a charming bundle, but pincushions and pen-wipers are not appreciated. Tettenhall sent a very pretty, as well as useful, bundle. The Llandaff ladies sent a splendid bundle; some of the prettier things I gave to Mr. Samuelson's and Mr. Carlson's children—they are too good for the natives—and one or two things I have kept for my own pet. Christ's Hospital, Hertford, sent a very nice little bundle; but the chemises and coloured print will be used as frocks; they would not like to wear any but white chemises. The guild of St. Philip's, Clerkenwell, also sent a bundle for the children.

Someone sent a box of thimbles, such nice ones that all the ladies on the station were eager for one. Most of them were exactly what we had been wanting for a long time—large ones; and we also wanted tailors' thimbles, as two of our boys from the Cape have been taught tailoring. Someone sent some pretty little bags containing needles, thimbles, cotton, and scissors. We gave one to each woman on the station. Someone sewed a few white pendant beads on a bit of red braid. E. gave it to the queen to wear round her neck, and she was charmed with it. Agnes begs I will send very great thanks for the little box. I shall give her a dress, as she wants one.

You should have seen us devouring your letters. Last Saturday, for instance, the post arrived about five o'clock. It was a very cold day, and I had a nice wood fire on the hearth in the draw-ing-room, and we sat with our feet on the fender, and my little work-table between us piled with letters and papers, and liter-ally drinking in every word; and were we not happy! We always get the letters that leave England on the 25th of the month, as soon as the mail arrives. A *Kafir* postman is sent to us.[2] He stays with us until we have answered our letters, and then takes back our mail.

Here is a true Zulu picture:—E. went into the kitchen on Sat-urday evening and found a poor cock suspended by a *rhim* (cord of ox-hide) from a beam; Agnes seated in triumph before it, plucking it, and sticking all the tail feathers into her hair; and Telesa, our other girl (and a *very* good one) playing to her on their instrument, which is like a string-bow. Agnes has a most warlike spirit; she is fall of fun, and E. and I find it very diffi-cult sometimes to keep from *chaffing* with her. She can be very *naughty* and *very trying*. The only way is then to tell her that she *troubles* me *very much*, and then she seems sorry. She is very quick; too much so, as she dashes about. It is a great trial to her when I make her pour the coffee out of the kettle *gently*. We make our coffee in the kettle. When the water boils we simply

---

2. From Rorke's Drift. Mr. Rorke was our postmaster; and his house, defended so gallantly by Lieutenants Bromhead and Chard, was our post-office through which all our letters to and from England passed.

put the coffee in and let it boil a little longer.

People think that the Zulus have things different from us, but they are most particular (the Christians I mean) to have things *like* us. The shirts must be like men's shirts at home, not with short sleeves. The women's chemises should be put into a band at the top and buttoned on a running string; but they like them best if they are high to the neck. Dresses also they like all in one, and a running string at the waist.

The names of the people here are as follows:—Usajabula and Christina (conceited and uppish), four children. Martyn[3] and Elizabeth (very nice), one child. Daniel and Fanny, two children. Sandulela and Anna, four children. Lydia (wife of Heber), eight children. William[4] and Lucy, just married. William Adam and Sophia, one child. Tobiana and Malia, one child. Henry and Blanche, two children. John Fea and Charlotte, Longcast[5] and Alice, one child. John Adam and his grandmother, old Mam. Dick (our carpenter). The lads are Usitemba (our boy), Peter, Alexander, Philip, Stephen, Jacob, Alfred. The girls, Agnes, Telesa, Lizzy, Yolande, Unoxuma. Martyn, William Heber, William Adam, and John Fea are the four E. spoke to on Sunday about a native ministry.

We have had so much to do that we have not been able to think even of silkworms. I think they will do here, and there is no lack of mulberries. But we must wait until the pressing work is over, I hope the vaccine is on its way from Dr. S. I want very much to vaccinate Edie. Have you a very nice young shoemaker? He would do well here.

I have thought it well to give the above letter just as it stands, as it will show to working parties what are the most useful and appreciated articles to send to a South African Mission. So many inquiries reach me from time to time upon what is required upon a Mission station for the natives, that the details of this letter will answer many such questions.

---

3. Later a native deacon.
4. *Ibid.*
5. Late interpreter to Lord Chelmsford.

CHAPTER 6

Station Life in Zululand

St. Mary, Zululand. June 26, 1871.

We seem to have perpetual summer, for although it is very cold in the mornings and evenings—June being midwinter—yet about 12 o'clock it gets delightfully warm; not warm enough, though, for a print dress. The children brought me some ice from the river the other morning. Don't, however, think that we have a noble stream at our feet. What is dignified by the name of river here is but a trickling stream. It is very cold getting up and going to bed, for we are having cold wind, and it blows up the verandah right into my room, and there is about a quarter of an inch space between the door frame and the wall, and the same again between the door and the door frame! The ceiling is covered with calico to hide the extremely roughly-made roof, much rougher than any barn.

I told you that E. has been speaking to four of the Christians here about becoming native clergymen. He spoke to them on Whitsunday, and told them he should talk to them again in a month, and that in the meantime they were to think of it with much prayer. Yesterday he spoke again. Only three were here, the fourth having gone with the waggon for wood to the forest. They spoke so nicely, and said that they felt they could not but think they ought to become teachers. So tonight E. begins to teach them further. One is a pure Zulu, another is a half-caste, and the other two are Hottentots.

I have just given away a bundle of clothes to all who work for us; a shirt, dress, and frocks for the children; and we have made three old women very happy with blankets, this being quite Christmas to them.

On Sunday E. confirmed the four boys who came from the

Cape, and three of the natives here. They sang the 24th Psalm in Zulu in procession. First the banner carried by one of the candidates for Holy Orders; then the boys in their cassocks, then the three others, then Mr. Robertson, then Hales carrying the staff, and then the Bishop. The recessional was to have been a translation of "*Put then thy trust in God,*" but I made a mistake, and began it before the service was really over, so we had one answering to "*Lord, dismiss us.*"

I have just performed the horrible and nasty feat of skinning a hawk. I had never done such a thing before, and when it came to turning its head inside out, I nearly gave it up. It is a beautiful little creature, white breast, grey wings and back, red eyes, and yellow legs.

I had a tooth out a few Sundays ago. A mason took it out for me beautifully! I wanted E. to do it, but he felt nervous. To show you that he is not bad at extracting teeth, a poor woman came last Sunday for some medicine to put in her tooth. She had had two out before by Mr. Robertson, and felt the pain was too great to have another out. I gave her the best I had, but this morning she came again and said she must have it out. Poor thing, she was very frightened, and begged to have her head held—a most unusual request. E. took it out in a moment, and she said that it was not half the pain of the others, it was done so quickly, although E. felt a little nervous at seeing the poor woman so nervous.

I have just got a charming brood of thirteen chicken. I am gradually getting up a stock; and Mrs. Walmsley sent me two turkeys the other day, such lovely silver-coloured ones. We have begun to make bricks; they made 2,500 today. My business was to keep the count. E. yesterday kept the floor of the brick-yard tidy, but he is very stiff in consequence, and has been writing all day.

Dr. Callaway[1] is coming up here. The Prince Cetywayo wants to consult him. He is an elderly man, and calls it an awful undertaking. People in Maritzburg know no more, perhaps not so much, about Zululand, than you do. They look upon it as some wild, unknown country over the border. The poor doctor may well call it an awful undertaking.

It is wonderful how perfectly safe one is here amongst these na-

---

1. Later Bishop of St John's, Kaffraria.

tives. One might walk with perfect safety through Zululand at night, and that is more than one can say of England. The natives are always most polite. Mrs. Robertson says that she does not like to feel that a man is walking behind her with his spears; but that is nonsense. They always carry two spears and two sticks, generally a shield as well. They never stir an inch without their spears and sticks except when they come into the verandah or into the house, then they are always left outside.

The natives are most inquisitive and curious as to our ways. Here is a specimen. E. always shaves even in a *Kafir* hut. He goes through that uncomfortable operation on his knees in front of a glass about the size of an orange, which generally refuses to be propped up. It was most amusing when I was with him upon that little excursion. Whilst we were dressing, four native women crawled into the hut, and, squatting on their heels, watched us most intently. When I combed out my long hair they were most astonished.

Of course on these excursions one 'goes to bed' in one's clothes, *i.e.* one lies on a grass mat with a blanket for a covering. Oh, how I ached after lying on the hard earthen floor for three nights! You would not have called my mattress at home hard after that. To show you how cold it is here, we sent a man to Mr. Jackson the other day. He did not arrive when they expected, and one of his men found him half dead in the cold, speechless and unable to move without help. I hear that many every year die of cold on the hills; they get sleepy, lie down, and never wake again.

The cold of this winter season, and the ill-built house in which we lived, brought on the cough referred to, which ended in an acute attack of pleurisy. For weeks Mrs. Wilkinson was unable to lie down in bed at night, and suffered great pain. It was a long and anxious illness in which no medical aid could be obtained. The assistance of Natal doctors was sought, but none could be induced to come up into Zululand. The many discomforts and privations, so greatly aggravated by the surroundings of a wild country and a rough life in which none of the comforts and conveniences of civilisation could be obtained, were borne—as all the other troubles and trials of her life—with the greatest patience and cheerfulness. It was always a leading feature in her character to make the best of things, however bad and dark they might be. When able to move about again it was with but a feeble step and exhausted strength. 'She was fearfully ill' wrote Mr. Robertson to friends in England.

St. Mary, Zululand. July 22, 1871.

The mail arrived last Friday. Our letters were only forty-nine days old from England. There is something very pleasant in expecting the post on Saturday, and looking over the hill for the old *Kafir* postman—from Rorke's Drift—in his red coat. I think that all the old army red coats are sent out to Natal, for the *Kafirs* wear them. In towns they are obliged by law to wear something, and these coats are nice and warm. A great many of our Zulus have them—not the Christians—though by far the greater number have simply their tails.

I have just come in from church, and E. delighted us by giving us an English service, and we sang hymns 311 and 325. We do so enjoy an English service, for we only have it on saints' days, and morning and evening with early celebration on Sundays.

I have been for a ride this afternoon. My stupid old *Kafir* horse took it into his head to roll; so down he went on to his side, fortunately on the side my legs were, so I jumped off in a minute, and did not get my feet entangled, fortunately. I shall never have a horse again like my dear old Abbot. I always ride now with fear and trembling, the horses stumble so. You do not find one in thirty *trot*, they *giffle*. We rode to see a cow and a young bull. We wanted the cow to kill for Dr. Callaway's dinner. We paid blankets, value 17*s.* 6*d.*, for the cow; and for the young bull, about two years old, we paid blankets value 11*s.*, and a three-penny knife on the top of the bargain!

I am buying a lot of grass for thatching the new house, and I have great fun with the old wives. I put up two stakes, five feet apart, and a string at the top, connecting them, four feet from the ground. Into this measure they bring their bundles. They try to put in the thick end of the bundles, but I push in the thin end. I cram and jam, they throw on lightly if they can, and we have great laughing over it, and then I give them some snuff, and they call me their mother. For this measure I give a cotton sheet, value 3*s.*

We have been hard at work the last month making bricks. E.'s work and mine has been turning and stacking them, for here, as soon as the bricks are made they are laid in rows upon the ground. When they begin to get firm we turn them, and in another day carry them off the ground, and stack them in rows. We have made 30,000. We make about 2,000 a day. One man makes them; but then we have twenty Zulus at work, some stamping the clay, some carrying off the bricks, some washing the forms. It is a busy scene, and one must work hard the whole time. I watched Mr. Carlson; he made eight in a minute invariably.

July 28.—You should see me at this moment. Seven girls at the window, and one man clamouring at me because they say I have given them too few beads for some grass. Two more men have arrived who cannot agree with me about the price of a bull!

We have been so delighted with a visit from Dr. Callaway. He says if he had known what a long journey it was he could not have come. He thought it was only two days from the Tugela, instead of which he found it seven, for he travelled slowly and came by the waggon track. He has this morning started with Mr. Robertson for Panda's *kraal*, and then they go on to Cetywayo. We had a dinner party last night of twelve! It is rather amusing because we cannot dress until we have dished up dinner—which was grand for Kwamagwaza.

We had a most splendid piece of sirloin of beef, about 16 lbs.—I cut it off the quarter of bullock myself!—two boiled chickens, and a ham; a plum pudding, open tart, and jelly, which any cook in England might have envied me. I had never made one before, but I followed dear M.'s receipt when she nursed A. S. at Lichfield in 1857. I had the bullock's legs to get the "neat's foot oil" for Mr. Hales, the carpenter, and then I found I had beautiful jelly, and we are well off here for lemons. You would have laughed so if you had seen our two girls, who ought to have been waiting at table, sitting in the drawing-room giggling. It has been so refreshing to E. to have an intelligent man like Dr. Callaway to talk with.

I shot such a beautiful little bird the other day; it had a long red beak, grey breast, and blue back and wings. E. fired and missed, so I was proud of "wiping his eye." E. has skinned it, and is sending it home, but a wretched rat last night ate off one foot and nibbled the wing. I have got two little pigs; it is the first litter, but still of course it is miserable. The father is Hampshire breed; we brought him up in the waggon in a small box when we came up.

Dr. Callaway intends returning to Natal on Monday week, and E. is going as far as the Tugela with him, and there meets Bishop Macrorie. I am so glad, for the change and a little talk with educated men will refresh him. As he says, we have many little daily worries, but we cannot get away from them, no one to ride over to see, or spend a few days with. We are always in the midst of our anxieties. But Dr. Callaway has told E. that they ought not to bring everything to him. If a boy refuses to work, or a man comes very late, or there is no wood to go on building, &c., all come to him, and this bothers him, as he cannot of course speak to them yet. Dr. Callaway says, "I won't have it; I won't hear them. I say, 'Don't come to me, I am too great; I don't see you: go to my man.'" It is very hard for a stranger to introduce discipline when for ten years there has been none. Of course the men don't like it, or you for introducing it. They like to go on in the old way of dropping in to work at any hour, and leaving off when they like.

August 2.—E. went off yesterday to SS. Philip and James station. He started yesterday morning at 10 a.m. on his thirty-five-mile ride. I hope he will be back on Friday, I being left in charge of the workpeople.

All the bartering, such as that of the cow, the bull, and the grass referred to in this letter, was done by Mrs. Wilkinson. She was inimitable at this. Shrewd and yet so cheery and full of fun with the Zulus, which they so fully appreciated. I used to hear shouts of laughter whilst these barterings were in progress, ending always by a solemn snuff-taking, all seated on their heels, and exclaiming with admiration, '*Mame, mame wetu! Inkosikazi, Inkosikazi yetu!*' 'Mother, our mother! chieftainess, our chieftainess!' In travelling she would always manage to get a better hut, and buy better and more food, than any of the party.

As soon as we off-saddled at a *kraal*, either during the day or for the night, she would go about amongst the huts and see what they had, and we would presently hear shouts of laughter and great bargainings going on which invariably resulted in her triumphant return at the head of a bevy of women and girls, bearing to the hut appointed for

79

us an abundance of food for ourselves and our horses.

St. Mary's, Zululand. Sept. 23, 1871.

Here am I, a poor disconsolate mate, left without E. for six weeks. He left on the 21st with Mr. Robertson, five native bearers, a white man who lives here, and three natives as hunters. They are going to travel through a splendid game country, so I hope they will not fall short of meat. He took a lot of coffee, tea, cocoa, sugar, bacon, cheese, and a quantity of rusks which I made for him, and which turned out a great success. I was determined he should not go without plenty of food, for of course he cannot live on *Kafir* food, although an excellent addition. He also took quinine and other medicine; but I hope he will require neither, for, as he is riding, Mr. Robertson has chosen a more northerly route to avoid the unhealthy district for horses,[2] and they will be at a higher elevation even than we are, so that I am not under the least anxiety as to his welfare; indeed, I think the change will do him good, for we have been here nearly a year, and of course we have had many anxieties, as everyone has, but we cannot go to a friend's house for a week and shake them off. He will go through quite a new country and have plenty of fun with the *hartebheests*, magnificent antelopes as large as an ox, besides quantities of smaller game. There are thousands of these *hartebheests*; how a sportsman would envy him!

I have plenty on my hands, for I am left head, and all the ploughing and sowing will have to be done whilst they are away, and a good many men to superintend. You cannot leave a black man very long to himself or he will make a mistake. But you know that I like farming. We have now six cows in milk, and I have begun to make butter. We had a treat this morning of first-rate Devonshire cream. Take four quarts of milk, put it on to the stove for an hour, never let it boil, and do not touch it for eighteen hours. I put the milk on about nine o'clock in the morning, and skim it about seven the next morning.

I have lots of poultry to see after, and I generally see the cows milked, for here if you want a thing done well you must see it done. I have this morning been putting in my first spring

2. The route between Zululand and Amaswaziland was not known by us when this was written. It was found that all the interlying districts were perfectly healthy for both horse and man.

vegetables, and now I shall soon see them coming up, and *such* coming up as it is! Not like the slow growth of spring things at home, but growing as they do in a hothouse, for we are seldom three days without a shower in summer, and then the warm ground is just like a hotbed.

Edie has such rosy cheeks, so different to the pale children at Durban and Maritzburg. I would not live in the former place upon any account. They several times last summer had the thermometer at 120° in the shade, whilst the highest we ever had was 86°, and the lowest 54°.

September 26.—The post came last night bringing a letter from the Bishop of Capetown to summon E. to assist at the consecration of the new Bishop of Grahamstown. I must write and tell him that I do not expect E. back before the first week in November, and as the mail leaves on the 25th, and the consecration is to be at Grahamstown on November 30, I do not think it possible he can go down.

The travellers are having lovely weather, not too hot; and there is a beautiful moon, so they can travel late and rest in the middle of the day. The waggon, with stores, only just arrived in time, for I had exactly one inch of candle left. I should have been reduced to burning a bit of wick steeped in bacon grease; wouldn't it have smoked and smelt? faugh! The princes are all so greedy for candles. Cetywayo is not satisfied unless you send him a box of twenty-five pounds, and that at 1*s.* 2*d.* per pound is no joke when you think of the trouble and expense of getting them up. We had to pay 7*l.*, for the load up to the Tugela, only three days' trek.

I told you of the fearful sickness amongst the cattle. They offered 7*l.* apiece for oxen the other day. We might have sold a lot but for our late lung-sickness, which has only left us enough for work. The usual price for an ox. is 3*l.* 10*s.* or 4*l.*

Both E. and I say we shall forget to speak English properly, for we have to adapt our language to our hearers. Mr. Carlson, a Norwegian, for instance, cannot always understand us, so we have to alter our speech to a still more simple form; and several of the people can speak a little English, and we have to talk sometimes Zulu-English.

I am so happy with my new horse; it is such a comfort to

think one can now get away from the station for an hour or so, for we have very few people to speak to because as yet we can understand very little. Zulus pass every day from all parts of the country, and the others can talk and hear the news, and what the Prince Cetywayo is doing, &c., but we have not even that little change. Some kind unknown friends sent me three stories—one a three-volume book, such a boon to everyone; only the worst of it is I am such a dreadfully quick reader.

October 18.—St. Luke's Day. Another letter from E. He wrote on the 5th, and was within three days of his destination, and said he hoped to be home in a month. He sent a lovely chestnut mare with the sweetest little foal, and a very pretty big pony mare with a beautiful roan foal nearly as big as herself. So now we are well set up.

October 26.—I was in the middle of R.'s letter when who should open the door and look in but E.! Fancy my delight and astonishment! He looked very brown, sunburnt, and dirty, but very well, and he has now recovered his usual appearance. I hope his visit has been useful. He was not allowed to see the young king of the Amaswazi, as Missionaries had never been heard of in that country, and all white people are supposed to be either Boers whom they hate intensely, or Portuguese come to seize slaves. I had a ride the other morning on my beautiful new bay, E. riding by my side, looking at it admiringly. When he bought her she was fat and beautiful. The *Kafir* was a whole fortnight bringing her, and had a bad saddle; the consequence is her back is in a dreadful state with two large sores, and so thin.

The route we took upon this first journey to the Amaswazi country was a very roundabout one, but we were anxious to consult a Mr. Rorke who lived at the drift house at the now famous 'Rorke's Drift' of the Buffalo River. On our way we visited Usihayo and stayed a night at his *kraal*. Next day, departing northward, our route lay immediately under the ill-starred Isandhlwana Hill. How little could we foresee, in passing under it on that bright, peaceful September morning, that it would one day be the scene of so terrible a tragedy, the undug grave of so many of our brave soldiers. This journey to Amaswaziland resulted in the foundation of the Amaswazi Mission, which has now its three promising stations.

The Rev. Joel Jackson must ever be considered the father of this

Mission. He was the first Missionary in that new and most interesting field, and most faithfully and earnestly has he followed up and developed the work amidst many real and great hardships, much isolation and discouragement. I baptised his first Swazi, a boy given to him, a young captive taken in war. We used a gourd as a font, and gave him the name of Harvey after the Bishop of Carlisle, who has always taken a warm interest in the Amaswazi Mission.

CHAPTER 7

Exploring the Amaswazi Country

St. Mary's, Zululand. Nov. 15, 1871.
We are now getting on capitally. Having become accustomed to the life, we know how to accommodate ourselves to it; and now we have no lack of food, which is not one of the least necessary things to comfort.

You will like to hear something of E.'s long-talked-of visit to the Amaswazi country. When Dr. Callaway was up here he said it was madness in E.'s attempting such a journey, and that most probably he would never return. But the good doctor is not accustomed to a Zulu life, and thought coming up here an awful undertaking, for no more is known of Zululand in Natal than in England, and living here is looked upon as quite a dreadful affair, as it is at home. I did not pay much heed, for I felt that the outing would do him good, and give him complete change of air and scene; but I insisted on his riding. This compelled them, as Mr. Robertson thought, to take a longer route in order to avoid unhealthy localities for horses.

I am very glad they did ride, for the horses ran home one night, and whilst a man was sent back for them E. was very poorly from having to walk in the hot sun. They went through a country very different from this, which looks as if the hills had been farrowed by a huge plough—large open plains of twenty miles breadth, with a mountain at the end, and the other side another large plain. That country seems to abound in game; in one day E. saw *hartebheests* (a kind of deer as large as an ox), ostriches, zebras, and gnus.

When they reached their destination, New Scotland, they found a good-sized but nearly deserted settlement. It was made by poor McCorkindale, of whom you may have heard. He believed it possible to make a port of Delagoa Bay, and so procure stores for the Transvaal country. The poor man had just gone down to the coast to meet his first cargo, which was to be conveyed up the river Pongolo in large flat-bottomed boats, when he was seized with fever and died. This happened about three months back, he having just before written to Mr. Robertson to ask him to go up and see him, and offering him land.

So E. started with Mr. Robertson, Hales (a carpenter), and ten native bearers. Mrs. McCorkindale received them most kindly, and continued to E. the offers made by her husband. E. immediately hired a house up there for a year; and Mr. Jackson, who has been at the new station, is going off at once to take possession. The advantages of this place are great; it is a piece of English territory on the borders of the Amaswazi country, so that the Amaswazy people can live there and do as they please with regard to their religion, without any fear of their being interfered with by their king and government.

E. went down to see the young King of Amaswazi Land, but English people being almost unknown in that country, he was not allowed to see him, however he saw all the old statesmen and chief instead. The only white men they know are either Boers who come and wheedle them out of their land, or Portuguese who come and steal their people as slaves. I said the settlement was nearly deserted; almost all the white people had gone up to the diamond-fields.

When on his journey E. bought and sent back to me three beautiful horses, a splendid bay horse, a chestnut mare with chestnut foal, and a bay mare with a roan foal. The horse is one of the nicest creatures I ever rode, so beautifully easy and free; it is such a comfort to have a horse to ride again. The day before yesterday we had a glorious gallop over the hills, getting such a blow from the sea. Although we are sixty miles off we can see it, and we feel that the wind from that quarter must be a sea breeze. It is not clear enough every day, but when it is visible we have only to go a dozen yards or so to see it.

We have been very busy putting in all our seeds and mealies, but, as E. says, it seems very strange to be singing the Advent Hymn with peaches as large as walnuts knocking against the windows of the church on one side, and ripe mulberries on the other. Talking of these fruits you must not imagine they are equal to those at home: the former are hard and not very good uncooked, though stewed they are delicious, and the latter are very small.

E. went yesterday with Mr. Robertson to see Cetywayo, intending to spend today (Sunday) with him. I expect him home again tomorrow, also the mail and the waggon, which is rather too much of a good thing in Zululand, waggon and mail arriving together; and this waggon will be especially delightful, for I expect our July box will be in it, also the harmonium. There is a small one here which E. has bought of Mr. R., and given to Mr. Jackson.

You may be surprised at E.'s moving Mr. Jackson when he had not long been at SS. Philip and James station, but he wishes to combine native work with work amongst white people. There are white people up at New Scotland who want a clergyman, and plenty of Amaswazi people; so by sending him there E. hopes to secure his services to this mission. Of course he knows the language well. If Mr. Jackson likes it we hope he will stay there. He has promised to try it for a year; but if he still wishes to go to the colony, E. will have a man ready to take his place; SS. Philip and James will be made a native mission station, and being only four hours' ride it can be well overlooked from this place.

E. will send a Christian from here to take charge of the buildings, and employ him to trade for cattle, &c., and every Sunday will send over one of his three candidates for orders to hold service there, preparing a sermon with them here. He has such a nice school now, four in the first class, who take it week by week to teach the second class, in which there are eight.

He keeps them three hours every afternoon except Saturday.

November 24—The waggons arrived, but no boxes from England; now we must wait till the middle of January for them. The mail, I hope, will come tomorrow. We have been having some very hot weather. The want of rain is beginning to be serious; the young mealie crop is being burnt up, I am afraid. We are going to have another wedding shortly, but I do not expect any more baptisms yet although we have two candidates under instruction. This will make the fourth wedding this year.

Upon the occasion of the visit to Cetywayo recorded in the foregoing letter we spoke to him very plainly and strongly upon the sure judgment that must come upon him and his land one day for the continued opposition offered by him, and some of his brothers and chiefs, to Christianity and civilisation. We spoke also of his unjust government and his cruel slaughters. But, as usual, he would not hear. He would sit for a while listening, or rather *suffering the speaker,* with a look like thunder upon his face, picking his inch-long nails in an impatient manner, and then would abruptly break off the conversation by asking about railways, telegraph, steamboats, the force of the English army, &c, &c.

A terrible sickness, which had decimated the cattle of Natal, and at one time threatened to exterminate them, now attacked the cattle in Zululand, as the following letter shows. It ultimately carried off 120 head of cattle at the station.

St. Mary's, Zululand. Dec. 4, 1871.

We have been rather uneasy again about our cattle; one ox died the other day, and the symptoms were identical with that disease which has killed so many of the cattle in the colony; and two more are sick. I think I mentioned the disease in the colony in my last letter as being worse than English lung sickness, there being no remedy; while we can inoculate for lungsickness. This other disease kills them in two days. But I am most thankful to say that both the sick oxen are better, so we trust it is not that dreadful plague. Not only the loss of the cattle, but the great expense of hiring waggons is entailed.

There have been two wrecks off Durban the last few weeks. Our agent was wandering on the beach, and picked up a piece of wood with "Zulu Mission" marked on it. He immediately went to the ship people and inquired if they had anything for us, and they said, "Yes, a box from the Ladies' Association;" and they gave up the things, five sacks full. When a ship is wrecked it is considered as lost, and everything is sold, so that they were very good to give us up the things. I do not quite understand this, unless it is that people generally insure their goods, and therefore cannot expect to receive both insurance and goods. I am so glad that it was only *that* box, and not ours from home, or the harmonium.

Martyn's wife Elizabeth is now Edie's nurse, so of course she will speak Zulu, which I had hoped might have been avoided. Since Tilly (the English girl) left we certainly have got on more with the language. We used to depend so much on her that we did not really try to understand what the people said. Now we have no one close at hand to interpret for us. I can make our own people, *i.e.* the native Christians, understand me, and generally make out what they want; but it is the raw Zulus, as we call the heathen, whom we cannot understand, nor they us.

Mr. Robertson says that they can all understand E.'s sermons, but of course he writes them at present, and when one is talking one forgets the pronouns, and the conjugation of the verbs, &c. E. does his sermons entirely himself. Mr. R. says he has the gift of picking up a language, and he is sure he would talk in a month well if for that time he would devote an hour daily to talking with the raw Zulus. But E. says he cannot understand them, and can only catch a word here and there, having no clue to what they are saying, although three times out of four it is certain to be about cattle. I hope next winter E. will take us down to the seaside in the colony, and we hope the Macrories will join us there. We are going to have a wedding tomorrow—a nice girl and a *very* nice boy, one of E.'s scholars.

St. Mary's, Zululand. Fest. St. Thomas, 1871.
The shortest day with you—our longest. A beautiful sunny day, but not in the least too hot, for there is a nice breeze. However cold a wind may be here, there is never that particular sting in it which yon experience at home. I *suppose* it is Christmastide, and that Monday is Christmas Day, but we don't talk about it. We shall have service, of course, we three lonely English people. We shall attempt a hymn, but as we are *minus* an harmonium, it having gone to Amaswazi Land with Mr. Jackson; it cannot be a lively one, I am afraid. I suppose feeling like this shows that at home we did not think enough of the festival, but thought too much of the family gathering. If so, we suffer for it now.

I have had rather a sharp attack of—so far as we can make out from our medical books—bastard pleurisy. I had no fever and no cough, so it could not have been the real pleurisy, but I had sharp cutting pains in my left side and under the collar-bone. It was worse at night, for I could not breathe when I lay down. It took every bit of my strength away.

The Robertsons started on their homeward journey on the 15th. They were obliged to leave early to allow for delays, for it is impossible to travel when it is raining, the waggon goes sliding down on one side in a most frightful manner, and then the rivers rise very quickly, and sometimes you must wait until they have gone down again; but they fall as quickly as they rise. Mr. Jackson and Mr. Hales have also started on their three weeks' trip up to the Amaswazi country. It will take them all this time because it is a new country to them, and they will have to find out the best waggon road. But E. says he can ride up there on any of our horses, sleeping three nights on the way.

Last Sunday E. sent over John Fea, one of his candidates for holy orders, to Empandhleni to take the service, it being the first after Mr. Jackson's departure. E. prepared a sermon with him. He had a congregation of nineteen. Martyn, another candidate, will go next Sunday, and William Heber, the third candidate, the next. Thus they will all take it in turns. E. will always prepare them through the week for the sermon. He came to me laughing last Saturday, having asked John Fea if he was not rather late in starting. "Yes," said John, "but I hadn't quite finished my sermon."

We have sent a married man to take charge of the station until such time as one of these three will be ordained, when he will take it. This is the first native station. These services will do them good, and sometimes E. or Mr. Carlson will go over with them.

With her usual unselfishness, Mrs. Wilkinson says, as will have been noticed in this letter, little about her illness, which was a severe and most trying one. For a long time she was only just able to move from the sofa to a chair and back again. When she got out it was only to walk a few yards at a time, and with a tottering step. It is possible that during this illness the seeds of that disease were laid which in August 1878 ended fatally. Whether this were so or not, it is certain that she never spared herself, but gave the best of her health and strength to do her Master's work whilst her day lasted.

The visits of the candidates for orders to the Empandhleni station referred to in this letter were very interesting at this time. I kept a diary of their experiences whilst taking these Sunday services amongst their heathen brethren. Under date December 24, 1871, I find this entry:

> Twenty-five present. Martyn distrustful of himself, being his first attempt; told me how he went aside to pray, and felt strength; and when he began to preach it all seemed easy to him. He told me before he went that he felt sure "God would help him through."

Under date Sunday, January 4, 1872, is this entry:

> Congregation of twelve to hear John Fea at Empandhleni. An old man and his son there; he talked much with John, and said he wished all the Zulus would become Christians. He knew they were wrong, because they hated and killed one another. If the prince (Cetywayo) became a Christian many would follow, he said.

> *Sunday, February 11.*—The old man John told me of last Sunday has had to fly for his life from Cetywayo's "*impi.*" People about SS. Philip and James much troubled, one man killed.

Under date November 12, 1872, the following entry as an illustration of Martyn's true interest in our work:

> 'Martyn came to me after school today, leading a nice-looking Zulu lad by the hand, and saying he had come to work. I asked, "Is he a friend of yours?"
> "No," he replied, with his nice smile, "but he may be one day," as much as to say he may be one of us one day. Prince Dabulamanzi (Cetywayo's brother), the great Zulu general who figured so conspicuously in the late war, also visited us about this time.

Under date Sunday, July 16, 1871, I have this entry:—

> Prince Dabulamanzi came, promised to send his four sons here to be educated; had been talking of it with the Prince Cetywayo.

> St. Mary's, Zululand. Jan. 12, 1872.
> I thought I should send this off by a man who was going down to the Tugela with eight of our oxen, but I found I could not write. We were obliged to send the oxen to our waggon, which was kept at the Tugela by the death of three oxen and the sickness of five others. Poor Miss R. was kept there also, in a most

beautiful spot, but in a dreadfully dirty house, consisting of two small rooms, inhabited by a man and his wife with a large family. I hope she will be home tomorrow or next day. It is a disappointment to me, this delay, for I was going to ride down with E. to Ondini to pay our respects to our new king Cetywayo. E. has got a beautiful present for him in the shape of a waggonette and harness and four mules. Of course now I cannot go, as Miss R. is not arrived, and E. *must* go tomorrow, for the carriage will have arrived.

Little Edie grows; she chatters away in Zulu, and we learn many words from her. Is it not ridiculous to think that we learn Zulu from a child that was not born when we landed in Africa? It is weary work longing for our letters; you cannot imagine what it is, our monthly post being the one little bright spot in our solitary life.

January 23.—E. and Mr. Carlson have just started to visit Cetywayo, and I am left in sole charge; but I have no difficulty in managing, for I am held in great respect by all the men. They know that the word of the "*Inkosikazi*" "chieftainess" is like the word of the "*Inkosi*" "chief," and I always hold the food, which is a great point with the Zulus. I have had great difficulty this year in getting my fields of mealies hoed. The Zulus generally do it, but this year, owing to the famine, they could not work; sitting still was all they could manage.

Fancy living on the roots of the white arum lily! It grows in great abundance in all the streams, and that is all many of the natives have to eat. We feed our pigs on it. The boy brings up huge bundles every day, and such magnificent flowers, all gobbled up. But now the new mealie crop is getting ripe. Whilst soft and milky they are delicious roasted in the cob before the fire.

What do you think I have done? prepared the "key" for taking out two poor creatures' teeth. I have never yet attempted to extract, but mean to practise privately on the next sheep we kill. John Fea is the dentist on the present occasion. He cannot get the girl's tooth out; he says, "it is very much tight in."

January 27.—E. is back from Cetywayo, who was very gracious, and so he ought to be, seeing E. took him so handsome a present.

Coal is found in great quantities in Natal; you can dig a whole waggon-load for 5s.; but in Durban it is 7l. or 8l. per ton; transport is so expensive. I have no doubt there is plenty near us if we only know how to look for it. As it is we have plenty of wood. Trees blow down, or I send a Zulu to cut one down and cross-saw it into lengths, and then send the oxen to drag it home, and the girls chop it up as they want it.

I think for one week I will keep a list of all the cases I doctor, and the medicines I administer. It will amuse you.'

As an instance of the way in which Cetywayo ruled his country I may mention an incident which occurred during my visit to him which is alluded to above. Cetywayo allowed a certain time every morning in which to hear the many and various cases brought to him from all parts of the country. No one *stands* in his presence. It is not etiquette to stand in the presence of a superior. I remember when we first landed in Durban, and were the guests of Archdeacon Robinson, being highly indignant at his *Kafir* man squatting down on his haunches in one corner during dinner instead of standing behind his master's chair. When I represented the apparent indecorum to the archdeacon he said, 'Oh, his position is one of entire respect; he would not upon any account be so rude as to stand in our presence when not attending to our wants.'

As deputation after deputation was presented to Cetywayo on this occasion, they approached him grovelling upon their hands and knees, and there remained prone before him, representing their several cases. I was standing with Mr. Carlson one morning during our visit in the king's presence, whilst he was listening to a case of witchcraft. He heard the case through to the end, but several times during the recital of it he yapped like a dog. Mr. Carlson, who, long resident in Zululand, knew the customs of the people well, turned to me and said, 'Do you know what Cetywayo means by making that noise?' I said 'No.' He replied, 'I think he means by it that not a dog is to be left in that *kraal*, all are to be destroyed.'

St. Mary's, Zululand. Feb. 9, 1872.

Owing to some disturbances in the north our postman was driven back, and we only got the mail yesterday. The consequence is, we must send down a special messenger to catch the outgoing mail of the 21st. And now I have not had time to answer your letter until now. In the first place a white man arrived to breakfast, and then I had to provide a better dinner. Then they came to say that Elizabeth's mother was much worse, and at twelve o'clock she died, and they wished her to be buried this evening. Of course there were many little things to do;—a pall to make, which I made of dark blue *selampore*, with a white cross of moleskin, and E. made an exquisite wreath and cross of blue hydrangeas and pink geraniums and white roses. Then the funeral at 5 p.m. So you see this has not been an idle day, for E. had to superintend making the coffin which we covered with calico.

One of our horses is sick. I am terribly afraid they will not live here, but I am thankful to say it is not my beautiful horse. Mr. Drummond arrived within thirty miles of this place about a fortnight ago, with a friend who was very ill with fever caught in the Amatonga country. He sent to us for medicines, &c., and we sent him a horse to come on here. The poor man was miserably weak. Mr. D. says he really thinks he would have died but for the timely arrival of our Liebig's extract of meat. They stayed with us for a week, and we nursed him nearly to full strength. Mr. Drummond[1] is the son of Lord Strathallan.

My mealies are splendid. I say *mine*, for at the planting season they were all away in Amaswazi Land, and I was obliged to superintend the work. I was told today that they had never seen such a crop before, so I am a proud woman. I cannot get any young ducks, but I have about ninety chickens, so I have something to do, as you may imagine, feeding them all. This is an unusually dry summer. Mr. Carlson, who has been out here ten years, says he never knew so dry a season. I am glad, for I don't like living in the clouds at all, but poor E. has been nearly distracted with his young hedges, which he has planted three times. I have a sow and nine young pigs. She had ten. I said to the Zulus that ten was not many, but they said it was "*iziningi*"—"many indeed."

Our beautiful harmonium has arrived. It is such a pleasure to us, for our services, especially the English, had been very dreary. It has eleven stops; in fact, it is quite like a little organ, with no harsh tones. What an awful fire at Chicago! I can realise it a little, for I have seen one fierce fire here, and you have no idea what a great fire is when there is a strong wind; it goes flying

---

1. He was killed at the Battle of Ulandi; his horse rushed with him into thick of the enemy, and he was never seen again.

up the hills at a terrible pace.

The Zulus are so handsome, and so well made, it is a pleasure to look at them; not like those hideous little creatures which are supposed to be Zulus in "the Net." We have a great deal to do for them in the doctoring here, and I am so sick of weighing and measuring medicines and making up pills. Two days ago I had three different people waiting for medicines, and this takes up a great deal of time, for we have to find from our books what the disease is. The other day a case was brought of a man who had a spear wound right through his body. Just fancy having to doctor such serious cases! He was bleeding internally. We sent him some medicine, and the bleeding soon stopped. I am sure that if one does one's best, with prayer, our imperfect knowledge is blessed to a very great extent. Today I have had two cases, one very like leprosy; the other a child with a very bad eruption on the head. I have begun the first with a good dose of potash, the second I washed in tincture of iodine. I have been doctoring this last for some little time, and it is certainly better. But all this takes up a great deal of time.

We have had such a beautiful altar-cloth sent us, red velvet superfrontal, and white silk frontal, most beautifully worked in silks and gold thread. We have had cross, candlesticks, and vases sent us. The first stones of the new church were drawn this morning. What we want most now are lamps, and we are perplexed as to the sort. We must have paraffin, and paraffin in Durban is just the same price as *colza* at home.

This letter will give the reader some idea of the strangely mixed work which missionaries are called upon to do in a far heathen country such as Zululand. The Christian Zulus thoroughly appreciated the care with which we conducted the funerals of their relatives and friends. There cannot be a more striking contrast than that between a heathen and a Christian funeral.[2]

---

2. I was enabled to mark this difference by close contact upon one occasion. I passed from a terrible heathen death, where the weeping and wailing for the dead, and the beating of the body upon the ground, followed by those weird cries at night on the lone hillsides to the spirits of their ancestors to send no more death, contrasted strongly with a native Christian funeral I was called upon to attend the next day. Mourners there were in this case also, but not mourning as those without hope; singing a funeral hymn at the open grave, and then going their way to talk over amongst themselves and compare the difference between death amongst heathens and the death of Christians.

CHAPTER 8

Station Life, and a Start For Amaswazi Land

St. Mary's, Zululand. March 26, 1872.
This has been a fearful summer for the poor Zulus, a second winter indeed, inasmuch as we have had no rain. All the crops, with the exception of those on the high lands, like ours, are entirely burnt up, and the people have only the mealie crop to depend upon. If that fails they must live on roots, &c., and starve. We, I am thankful to say, have a good crop. I think the great dryness of the air for now nearly a year has been very trying to everyone.

E. is now preparing eight candidates for confirmation and three for baptism. We had by this mail such a charming letter from dear Bishop Tozer. Samuel Speare has been ordained subdeacon, and is now in charge of a little mission station on the island of Zanzibar. He has all the unbaptised boys under his charge. The bishop speaks of him in the very highest terms.[1] Our three candidates for Holy Orders are going on very steadily. They go to SS. Philip and James every Monday in turns. One has just returned; he had a congregation of 17. This is nice, is it not?

We have just had a thunderstorm, such rain, a real tropical rain; I never saw the like, but only lasting a short time. The thatch is so dry that our roof is leaking everywhere. I became aware of it in my bedroom first by a little stream running down the back of my neck.

---

1. The life of this excellent young man has been published by the Society for Promoting Christian Knowledge, under the title of *A Suffolk Boy in East Africa*. As good and true a life as ever was lived, it must do good wherever read.

It was indeed, as stated in this letter, a fearful summer for the poor Zulus; the famine was so sore in the land that many had to live upon roots. Poor creatures would come with little baskets not much larger than thrushes' nests, and hold them out to be filled with seed of the Indian corn, promising two or three days' work for each little measure. We had to send a waggon to the German settlement of Luneberg upon the Pongolo, a distance of 400 miles there and back, for a load of Indian corn. Upon its way back the chief Matyana stopped it and took out almost by force, though he did it under cover of friendship and acquaintance with us, a sack of Indian corn, and gave an ox in return.

This was but poor payment that year. Corn was priceless. When the drought had continued long we offered prayer for rain in the little church at Kwamagwaza one Sunday. During evening service the rain fell in abundance. The news spread far and wide that the bishop had 'made rain.' A white man who came next day said he heard the Zulus talking of it by the way. It seemed to impress them, since all their best rainmakers had failed, and Cetywayo had threatened them with death. 'Ah, foolish people!'

St. Mary's, Zululand. April 14, 1872.
I am thankful to say that Miss R. is better, though still very weak. She has, I believe, been dangerously ill with inflammation, but my efforts to relieve her were blessed. How fearfully ignorant one feels in cases like these! I could only pray that what I did might be blessed. Poor thing, I salivated her I am afraid, too much for her comfort. We gave two hot baths, and then the inflammation flew to the throat and mouth, which were in a terrible state of ulceration. One day she was very exhausted, and I gave her Liebig and port wine every half-hour. I had a hard week, as you may imagine, with Putu only a month old, who at that time took it into her head to keep me active all night.

I told you of the dreadful drought, but that *our* mealies were very good. Well, what do you think? Our wicked herd-boy forgot to shut the cattle *kraal*, and the whole herd, about one hundred, came out and walked into my mealie garden. Oh the havoc they made! not so much from eating as from trampling down the mealie stalks; and they were not ripe, so could not be picked. The next day we had a terrific gale of wind and rain, which laid the whole crop "even with the ground." Adams says he never remembers such wind and rain to last so long. It killed our poor dear sow. I found her lying stretched out in the sty. Adams is now going to stay with us a month to make the bricks, and then he is going to take us down to the sea. I am so glad, for it will save E. all the trouble during the journey. We shall spend our Sunday, as we go, at Mr. Samuelson's, for E. is going to consecrate the church,[2] and hold a confirmation. We shall then go on and spend two or three days with Cetywayo. We shall take the horses with us, but we shall not be able to bathe, there are so many sharks, and the rivers also close by are full of alligators. Our tent will be our house whilst we are away. It is such a nice one, with two porches.

They have tremendously big canvas towns at the diamond-fields. This great population, we find, has raised the price of everything in Natal. Fancy E.'s horror, when he wrote for the iron roofing for the church, to be told there was not a sheet in the colony, all had gone to the diamond-fields! Our agent in Durban was going to make forty tons of jam to send to the fields.

Our garden is beginning to look winterish, that means all the flowers a huge size. We shall cut them down gradually, for they never cease flowering. They do not, however, flower so profusely as at home; poor things, they are at it all the year round.

J. F. has taken rather alarm at my writing that the Amaswazi were suspicious of E., since the only white men they knew were Boers, who cheated them out of their land, and Portuguese, who take their young people for slaves; and fears that E. may share Bishop Patteson's fate. E. had written for a Government letter introducing him to the Amaswazi. The same mail brought word that there was a difficulty in the way, so E., taking a hint from what J. F. says, is going to write to Lord G. on the subject.

There is a rumour in Natal that gold has been found in Zululand, and that the English are going to take possession of the country. I only hope they will let us know first, that we may scuttle away as fast as we can. But of course it is only a rumour, they have nothing to talk about just now.

What would you think of sleeping on the grass under a waggon in a terrific thunderstorm with torrents of rain? Adams has just returned from the bush, where he has been cutting scaffold-

2. This pretty little church was entirely destroyed during the war.

poles for the church, and as he was coming home that was what befell him; he was not able to make a fire. Mr. Jackson writes from Amaswazi Land that he went a three days' journey to visit the young king. There is a dreadful famine in that country also, and one day after travelling in a burning sun, all he got for his supper was one roast mealie cob. Another day, after travelling all night, he got a cup of beer, and no breakfast next morning. That is something like hardship, is it not?'

It has been thought well to give this full account of the dangerous illness of Miss R., a lady who was attached to the mission. It will serve to show what illness is when it befalls one far away in the wild, and how much additional strain it puts upon already overstrained heads, hearts, and hands. Serious illness brings anxiety enough at home, where skilful medical aid, good servants, and every civilised appliance and luxury is obtainable; what it brings without any of these, they only can tell who have experienced it.

St. Mary's, Zululand. May 16, 1872.
On Monday I start, D.V., with E. for the Amaswazi country on horseback. He says it will be hard work, but I am not afraid. We go first to the king's (Panda). One of his daughters is ill; she is subject to fainting fits, and having been relieved by some *sal volatile* which E. sent her she thinks him a great doctor, and begs he will go to her. She is a very superior person, and at heart a Christian, though if she were openly to profess it she would be immediately killed. She never talks in the Zulu fashion, but is always inquiring and asking intelligent questions. We shall sleep the first three nights at Norwegian mission stations, riding about forty miles a day, and the last two nights in *Kafir* huts. We take Martyn and William, the two Hottentots, both clever little fellows.

How shocking was the murder of Lord Mayo! I think we are safer here than in most places. The English are held in such respect by the Zulus. They hate the Boers; dislike, or rather hold in contempt, the Germans; and fairly like the Norwegians. The Zulus firmly believe that the English have eyes at the back of their heads, but change when they come into this country.

Adams is hard at work making 45,000 bricks for the church; such a busy scene, running backwards and forwards with the bricks, stamping the *udaka*, or clay, turning the bricks, &c. Last

98

Sunday E. admitted John, William Heber, and Martyn to be readers, and on Sunday he is going to hold a confirmation. I think he will have eight after he has weeded them.

Our garden is still very productive, owing to the late rains. We have quantities of potatoes, Brussels sprouts, cabbages, and a few cauliflowers, so we are not reduced to pumpkin, as we were this time last year.

Whit Sunday,—We have just had our confirmation, six girls and three men. We had holy communion afterwards, at which twenty-three natives communicated. I must finish this off, for we hope to make an early start tomorrow for Amaswazi Land. Kitty has a sore back, so we have sent to borrow a nice black mare of a chief who lives about fifty miles off; but that is only considered a day's ride from here. Perhaps when we come back we may be able to send more letters to catch one of the many mails that now come and go from Durban.

This was the last time we saw King Panda. He was then old, feeble, and withered. Lying upon his mat, and almost forsaken save by a few humble attendants. Cetywayo was practically the reigning monarch, and had been so for several years. Yet old Panda's eye was still sharp and keen. He received us most courteously, and said he would give me an ox if I cured his daughter. When I declined his offer, and told him that I had not come to attend his daughter for what I could get, but as an act of friendship and goodwill, he seemed pleased and astonished.

Ubatonyile, the daughter who was ill, was a most excellent person. Although a heathen, she was known to be a Christian at heart. The Norwegian missionaries, who had a station near Kanodwengu, Panda's *kraal*, where she lived, took great pains with her, instructed her daily, and taught her to read. She could say the *Creed* and the *Lord's Prayer*, and was particularly fond of the *Te Deum*. She hated the heathen life which she was compelled to lead, and was always longing to escape to the colony, where she might exercise openly the faith which she believed.

She once asked a trader to secrete her in a load of skins he was taking to Natal, but the attempt dared not be undertaken. Had she been caught on the Zulu side of the Tugela, Cetywayo, her brother, would have killed her. One good issue of the Zulu war has been the giving of liberty of conscience in religious matters, not only to this good woman, but to thousands of others like-minded with herself, formerly held in a cruel thraldom by Cetywayo.

St. Mary's, Zululand. June 18, 1872.

You will see by the beading of this letter that we have returned safe and sound after our 470 miles ride. I enjoyed the expedition immensely, and did not knock up, and have to be nursed as E. predicted. He knocked up instead, and was ill at a good German missionary's house. However, after that he was quite well, and on our journey home said he felt equal to riding to Capetown. I don't think Amaswazi Land will be considered such an unknown country now that a lady has been up there. We rode home in four days, fifty miles a day, sixty-six the last day. Our horses did it splendidly in spite of sore backs, but the last day their feet were terribly tender from going over a very stony pass, a great climb up big rocks, down which they had to jump on the other side. It sometimes happens that your horse nearly falls on to you. Sometimes we did ride down awful places, especially into rivers, down steep banks, where the horses had to jump down from one ledge of rock to another; I used often to cry out.

It is very hard, I can tell you, lying on a single blanket in a Zulu hut; it makes one's bones ache; and cockroaches running all over you is not pleasant. But we got on very well, and dear old Martyn took such care of us. He got a horrible fall one day. E. was riding on in front, and I next, and Martyn behind. My horse partly cleared the ant-eater's hole, but went in with his hind legs. I called out, and the next moment heard an exclamation. I looked round, and there was Martyn going over his horse's head, which made a complete somersault over him. These holes are horrible things, and very often entirely hidden by the long grass. They are about the size of fox earths, only perpendicular. The first thing he said when he had shaken himself was, "I am awfully glad that *Inkosikazi* did not get this fall." We saw one day a splendid herd of *hartebheests*, about forty;[3] another day a herd of zebras: it was a little too early in the winter to see the ostriches.

On Sunday three girls arrived here, having run away from one of the princes. They are the children of great people. We sent to tell the Prince Umahanana at once, which is the proper thing

---

3. This was at Isipezi Hill, a fine position for reconnoitring during the Zulu war.

to do; and today two men arrived to take them away, but they refused to go. The men said, "Well, then, the prince will send an '*impi*' (band of spearmen) to take them by force." So E. said he would appeal to Cetywayo, and told Mahanana to wait for his answer, which E. would abide by. Whether the prince will do so or not I do not know, but I am rather dreading the arrival of this "*impi*" tomorrow, for E. has ridden down with Martyn to Cetywayo. He means to sleep at Mr. Samuelson's tonight.

Upon the horseback journey to Amaswazi Land an incident occurred which will give an idea of the cool self-possession and ready courage with which Mrs. Wilkinson met every exigency of her African life. We arrived one evening at a *kraal* upon the wild border-land beyond the Pongolo River, amongst the hills which lie neither in Zulu nor Amaswazi Land—a kind of Cave of Adullam,—where lived the discontented and unruly, and to which range of hills Umbelini in the late war betook himself, and gathered these discontented together. The headman of the *kraal* was absent upon our arrival, but the 'young men's hut' was cleared for our use, and, into it we crept and established ourselves for the night: it was cold and wet, and we were glad of the shelter.

Late in the evening an ill-conditioned young fellow with a bad countenance entered the hut, and spoke very insolently, demanding our right there, and bidding us turn out. I told him that the hut had been assigned to us, and bade him begone. He went out muttering, and we heard him in hot dispute with those who had given us the hut. Next morning we paid what was usual for the hut, and were up-saddling, when this young savage came up behind Martyn, and snatching away his blanket, ran with it up the rocks behind the *kraal*. I told Martyn to go on quietly saddling up, and that we would get the blanket before we left. I then went up the rocks, where I found my friend confronting me upon a ledge of stone, flourishing his *knobkirrie*, and daring me to come further. I parleyed with him, but to no effect, and not wanting to get a broken head, returned to the horses.

He soon came down, and going to his hut for his spears, joined the group which had now gathered in considerable numbers about us. Stepping round quietly behind one of the horses, Martyn seized the appropriator of his blanket, and after a short struggle they fell to the ground. The encounter was the work of a minute, but seeing Martyn beneath his adversary, and apparently being strangled by him, I came to the rescue. The young savage now turned upon me, and we became locked in anything but an affectionate embrace; his body, plentifully besmeared with grease, anointing a new riding coat with most unpleasant and unsanctified ointment. Mrs. Wilkinson, not knowing what use this young firebrand might make of his spears, now watched her opportunity, and creeping up behind him adroitly snatched them out of his hand, and threw them over into the cattle *kraal*. At this moment, when things were looking unpleasant, and we knew not what part the others would take in the affray, the headman's voice was heard in the distance storming away like a gathering thunderstorm: 'How dare one of his people lay hands upon the white man in his own *kraal?* Was the white man a dog, that he should be so treated?' The matter was now soon put right, the missing blanket restored, and the warlike young gentleman sent about his business very crestfallen and with his tails (monkeys' tails worn behind) closely tucked between his legs.

A year afterwards, when near this same *kraal*, at the time of the annual war dance, I met a band of young warriors on their way to the king's place. I stopped and spoke to them, and then recognised amongst the company, in full war attire, my sturdy antagonist of last year. 'Ah!' I said, 'I think I have seen you before. We don't easily forget those in Zululand who treat us badly.' 'Yes,' he replied, 'but it is well to remember the good we have received, and to forget the evil.' This was a just rebuke, and one thoroughly characteristic of the Zulus, who, though they can hit hard, are ever generous to forget and forgive.

The visit of Prince Mahanana to our station to take away his three girls was a serious matter, and might have ended with very serious consequences. He was very angry and overbearing upon this occasion, and threatened with his forty followers, who were all armed, to break into the station if Mrs. Wilkinson did not give up the girls. For a long time she refused, upon the plea that I had ordered them to be kept till my return. At last an experienced white man upon the station, and long resident in Zululand, advised her to yield. She did so at last under protest, and upon this condition. She told Mahanana in presence of the girls that if he ill-treated them for having run to us—and they are often almost beaten to death for such an offence—and should run to us again, we should do what we could to assist their escape into Natal, and then he would never get them again.

This they much fear, since Zulu girls are all worth their price in cattle, and are sold, often against their will, to some rich old tyrant. To escape this lifelong hateful slavery they will often run to one or other of the mission stations, and beg us to pay the cattle for them and adopt them as our children. I know no more touching feature of our work than this. These poor girls will throw themselves on the known justice and mercy of Englishmen whom they have never seen, feeling that we shall treat them honourably, and give them a free and welcome home amongst our native Christians, with whom they eventually intermarry according to their own choice. The young Christian native works to earn the cattle we have paid for the girl of his choice, and so returns them to us.

On this occasion Cetywayo advised my sending the girls hack to Mahanana at once. They were 'great people,' he said, belonging to the 'royal house,' and if he gave me leave to keep them it would get him into trouble with his brother. There was, however, no occasion to send them back; when I returned I found Mahanana had been to the station, and, as related, had taken them by force. Cetywayo was very gracious upon this occasion, as he always was *when he got his own way*. He gave me a very fine ox, and said, 'Don't eat it here, take it home with you. When white men get an ox, they like to eat it with their wives, I know.'

St. Mary's, Zululand. July 29, 1872.

We have had such severe loss amongst our bricks. Just as Adams had finished making 45,000, and was stacking them on the kiln, preparatory to burning, it began to pour with rain, and never ceased for four days and five nights. Half the bricks were entirely spoilt, and we have had to make them over again. This rain was a most unusual thing, and now we have just arrived at the same state we were in before the rain came. We are all working hard stacking. Two nights ago it began to rain again; E. jumped out of bed, the bell for work was rung, everyone came, and down they rushed with lanterns, for it was pitch dark, and were at work there for three hours.

E. stood in the middle of the brick-field holding up the lanterns on high, and so lighting the people who were covering the bricks with grass. The kiln was covered with the tent hammocks, waterproof sheets, mats, &c. We shall not be happy until the bricks are burnt. E. keeps groaning because it has delayed so long the opening of his school, and he feels certain his pupils are forgetting all he has taught them. They cannot come even in the evenings, they are too tired.

On Saturday we had a harvest thanksgiving service. We decorated the church with mealies in the cob, *amabele* (another kind of corn), and pumpkins, with flowers. Afterwards we had a feast, killed a cow, and had games.

We have had a quantity of lemons this year. E. counted on one tree 200—such fine ones,—would sell at home for threepence apiece. The orange trees are not old enough to bear, but a missionary near us sent us two sacks full the other day—magnificent ones,—such as you would only see in Covent Garden. I have made lemon marmalade; it is just like orange, you would not know the difference. We have seen great quantities of snow since I last wrote; it was on hills about forty or fifty miles off, the hills about Rorke's Drift. So you can imagine how much there must have been for us to see it at that distance with the naked eye. A friend writes from the Colony, "The snow is lying all over the hills, and the wind blows bitterly over them; we have plenty of oranges, but it is too cold to eat them."

Another girl, and woman with her baby, have come to us. After some difficulty we have got the girl by paying ten head of cattle for her, and now she is our absolute property. The woman's husband was killed a little time back as a wizard because a little buck jumped into Cetewayo's *kraal*, and they said it was an evil spirit sent to do him harm. Seven others were killed at the same time. The girl is, I should think, about seventeen; and rather old to have to manage, but they have a great sense of obedience to their lawful chiefs.

Our other girl, Telesa, who has been with us ever since we have been here, is such a good girl. For the last six months she has had all the work to do, and has done it well, housemaid, parlourmaid, and cook. I give her the meat and vegetables, and then she will entirely cook the dinner herself. She sees when the bread is getting low, and mixes and makes it herself, also the butter. She is far better than many an English servant. I am afraid I shall soon lose her, as she is to be married. That will make the fifth marriage since we have been here, so that we have quite a little village. We have now at the station thirty-seven adults and sixteen children, besides three families in other places. Then we have about ten more preparing for baptism.

E. and B. used to say that I should not do for Africa, because I was so dainty. I used to reply, "When I can get the things I like,

I take them; when I am in Africa, and can't get them, I shall take what I can get." And E. says I have certainly carried out my word. I have drunk my coffee without milk and sugar, *and said never a word.* We had quite exhausted our stores, and had no sugar in anything for a month before the waggon came up. I saved a little for the children's food, and they have always had plenty of milk.

In the heavy rain we lost four calves, and losing a calf here means the cow refusing to give milk, so we have been short. In a few days two cows will calve. I have got such a glorious fat pig, and a little one also which I put in, and he has become a little roly-poly on the others' leavings. I have seven, which I must fatten young, for I have no food for them. Our horses are all well. E. is going to break in one of the young ones. It is not, however, a good place for horses, they get poor; the pasture is not rich.

The unfortunate woman whose husband was killed upon a charge of witchcraft, lost many of her relatives at the same time. She herself was badly wounded and left for dead. In the evening recovering consciousness, she crept away into the bush with the little infant tied in a skin on her back, the daughter escaping with her. For many weeks they wandered about in the bush, afraid to show themselves, and living as best they could. At last, remembering what they had heard of the kindness of missionaries to natives in distress, they had resolved to make for some mission station, had found their way to us, and begged our English mercy and protection. This we are, of course, always ready to extend to distressed natives as far as we may be able to do so. We took in these people knowing they would soon be traced to us by their owners, all females in Zululand belonging to next of male kin.

In about a fortnight a company of armed men arrived to take them away. The woman begged us not to allow this; 'They will kill me,' she said, 'when they get me over the hills out of your sight: they speak fair to *you* because you are white people.' The girl stood up bravely and said, 'Kill me here if you please on the white man's place, but I will never go with you.' We then reasoned with the men, but they would not hear, and we thought all hope of saving these poor creatures was at an end.

We were just about to break up the '*indaba*' when Mrs. Wilkinson said, 'Do let us make another attempt.' We then represented to the men that the girl was of a high spirit, and that if they took her away by force she would doubtless escape from them and fly into Natal, and thus they would lose her value in cattle. This seemed to impress them, and they at last consented to take ten head of cattle from us for her.

Upon such occasions we always execute the transaction in the presence of witnesses white and black. We ask the girl if she wishes us to adopt her, we ask her owners if they consent. If favourable answers are returned on both sides we pay the cattle, and she becomes our adopted child. From that moment she attaches herself most loyally to us, looks up to the missionary and his wife as chief and chieftainess, to whom she brings all her joys and sorrows. We give her work in the house, or in some house on the station. She comes to school, she attends the church services, she moves about amongst our native Christians, who henceforth become her daily companions.

We put no religious pressure upon such girls. But sooner or later they are sure to come and ask us to prepare them for baptism, and sooner or later some young Christian lad comes and asks if he may make advances towards our adopted child So-and-so. If we think the match eligible, we consent; but the young Zulu lover is told that since we gave ten head of cattle for his lady love, we require the same at his hands. This exercises a most wholesome influence over the young gentleman. He has to work hard and steadily for several years before he can earn so many cattle. All the while we have him under our thumb, and if we see him tripping in his conduct, have a string always at hand by which to keep him in the right path.

Thus he serves for his Rachel, and I dare say they seem but a few days for the love he bears unto her. We generally relent when the ninth beast is paid, and allow the other to come in after the marriage; and this last one, I need not add, comes in very tardily. However, if the boy has done well, and we like him, we generally give it in; it comes as a kind of christening present to the first baby. Thus another little Christian household springs up in our midst, and so out of the very violence of the king and chiefs towards their people the church and kingdom of Christ grow. '*The fierceness of man shall turn to Thy praise.*'

Here is an instance of the entire trust we repose in these good Zulu girls, of whom I cannot speak too highly. We used to give them the key of our store-room, which was furnished with all kinds of mixed stores, like a village shop, and they were placed in charge of all. Of this they were very proud. Honesty is a bright feature in Zulu character. One afternoon, when the station is always quiet, all being out employed in field or garden work, I took my duplicate key and went into the store for something. Telesa happened to come into the kitchen which adjoined the store, and thinking that a stranger was there, rushed in like a young tigress, bristling with a righteous wrath, and exclaiming, 'Who is it that dares to enter my store?' When she saw me she covered her mouth with her hand, after the manner of Zulus when abashed, and went out.

I married the poor girl, whom we were enabled to save with her mother, to one of our young native Christians whilst we were upon a journey in the Transvaal. We were hurried in starting the morning of the marriage, and were therefore unable to give them the usual and much-prized marriage feast. The waggons had already started on trek before the marriage ceremony was ended, and I was obliged to send them off quickly on foot to pick the waggons up immediately upon its conclusion, we following on horseback. We did not do this, however, before we had wished them God-speed, and had put a quarter of a sheep upon the bridegroom's spear, with which he trotted off, *the wedding breakfast hanging over his shoulder, and his bride by his side!*

Poor things, we afterwards heard that they did not pick up the waggons for three days, and had to pass that portion of their honeymoon on the open *veldt*, sleeping beneath the stars of heaven. These, however, are small matters to Zulu brides and bridegrooms. They are reared in hard cradles, and often rest in cruel graves.

The following is Mrs, Wilkinson's account of Mahanana's demonstration with his *impi*, in a letter written at this time:—

Well, we did have an army whilst E. was away, and headed by the prince himself. Before he came a man arrived from him to say that he was now ready to treat with the bishop for the girls. I had them locked up. This was his trick to try and lure them out, and in half an hour one of our men rushed in to say the prince was coming. So I locked the kitchen, and then went and faced the prince. He was dreadfully angry, and began shouting "Open, open," and all his men also, thumping meanwhile at the door. There were about forty of them, armed with spears and shields, and they surrounded the house.

Mr. Carlson and I got the prince into the drawing-room and tried to reason with him, and make him wait for the bishop's return with Cetewayo's answer. But he would not, and every minute kept turning to me to open the door; but I paid no attention, and attacked him again with some other argument. At last it seemed quite evident that if I did not open he would break his way in, and then the girls would have been cruelly treated. Besides, it would never have done to have had the bishop's house forced. So after making him promise he would not hurt the girls either here or at home, I gave them up.

When E. got back he said I had done quite right. Cetewayo had received him most kindly, but said that if he kept the girls he would get into a great trouble with the king; and he, the prince, would get into trouble also, as these girls belonged to the royal house. E. was with him an hour (a long time to be with Cetewayo). When he came away he gave him an ox.

CHAPTER 9

Sickness, Famine, and the Gathering of the Zulu War Storm

St. Mary's, Zululand, September 22, 1872. Martyn is such a good fellow. He is a Hottentot, and has a charming wife. He sleeps in the house when E. is away. At this moment he is sitting by my side learning to write. I do not know what E. would do without him, he is quite his right hand. He can speak a little, or rather I should say fairly, in English. He is slow at his work, but the perfection of neatness and exactness. He has a very good influence on the station.

I have plenty on my hands now they have all gone to Amaswazi Land, for we must plough now the rains have come, and all the seed must be in before they get back. I have also draining operations to superintend, and a cattle *kraal* in course of building; but you know I like outdoor work, and hate kitchen work. I have all the wages to pay. We do not give them money, but they come every Saturday and take what they want in either blankets, a kind of blue cloth, beads, picks, knives, &c. It takes up a good deal of time serving them. As the waggons have not arrived from the colony, I am almost out of all kinds of barter goods.

The Zulus smoke a kind of plant which acts like opium, makes them stupid, and sometimes mad. E. has now made a law refusing to admit any to confirmation or Holy Communion who continue to smoke it, and all the clergy agreed with him. They may smoke as much tobacco as they like.

The many and various works to be ordered and overlooked upon the station were always placed in Mrs. Wilkinson's hands when she was left in sole charge; and it was not only found that she managed them all as well, but very much better than anyone else. She found little if any trouble in making the Zulus obey her. They worked for her readily and cheerfully, for she was always ready and cheerful in helping them and making them comfortable.

It was quite enough to make one like the natives to see the way they would watch her and look at her, as she gave the orders to them, with a mingled expression of admiration and comical wonder that a woman—a sex so looked down upon by the Zulus—should have such power and authority. They would sometimes put their hands over their mouth, and then burst out into the merriest round of laughter, exclaiming, '*Oh! Inkosikazi yetu, Inkosikazi impela yena*' ('Oh! our chieftainess is a chieftainess indeed'), she herself laughing as heartily as any of them.

> St. Mary's, Zululand, October 1, 1872.
> The waggons have not arrived yet from the colony. Our waggon has been waiting at the Tugela two months! The oxen will have become fat, that is one consolation, for the pasture down there is splendid. . . .
>
> *October 15.*—I am going to give the native children a feast tomorrow in honour of little Edie's birthday, and they are all nearly wild with excitement at the prospect. We have had another three days' rain; it is always cold then. Last night I was shivering, for the rain was driving in at my door; and now it is an exquisite morning, everything growing as in a hotbed. I don't think even changeable England can beat this. . . .

Some idea will here be gamed of the difficulty of getting supplies up into the Zulu country even in times of peace, the uncertainty of engagements being kept, the impossibility of communicating with civilisation outside in the colony quickly or regularly. In this instance our waggons were kept waiting at the Tugela River two months for waggons expected from Durban bringing our food and stores for the half-year. What the difficulties of transport must have been in provisioning our army during the late war cannot be imagined. I have letters before me now written about this time; one reports, 'We are all in a dreadful state for want of boots.'

Another reports:

We heard from a gentleman the other day, living on the other side of the Tugela, that he had one hundred tons of sugar waiting to be taken to Durban, but that although he was offering to pay 3*l*. 10*s*. per ton—it is only two days' waggon journey—he could not get it moved.

St. Mary's, Zululand, October 16, 1872.
Just now it is rather unhealthy here. I had an attack of fever about a fortnight ago. It is called fever here, but it is intense chilliness while the body is hot. I have been nursing our mare; she is so ill, owing to an overfeed of mealies. I have just poured down her throat gruel and milk with ginger and iron. Her little foal is so tame, we feed her with milk.

Our church is finished at last, and very, very nice it looks. The altar stands a considerable height above the rest of the church. It is planned like Rickinghall—a 12-inch step into the chancel cut into two 6-inch steps in the centre; then stalls on each side; two more 6-inch steps, and one 4½-inch. There is a triple lancet at the east end; the Crucifixion in the centre; Simon the Cyrenian bearing the cross on one side, and Ebed-melech the Ethiopian taking Jeremiah out of his dungeon on the other; at the west end, over the door, the baptism of the Ethiopian eunuch; and three lancet windows on either side of the church, filled with cathedral glass. The flooring is asphalt, but cemented within the chancel. All the buttresses are dressed with cement, and Mr. Jackson, who did not know it, said, "Where did you get your stone from?"

I think we shall soon have a telegraph to Aden, so we shall be more in the world. The "Donald Carrie line" always arrives at the Cape in twenty-four days, and Durban in thirty. We had a long letter from Miss Tozer at Zanzibar by this mail. She gives a deplorable account of the bishop's health. Sam Speare is home by this time for a year, and hopes to go back in deacon's orders. Our boy Frank, the Zambesi boy, has turned out very well. He, and one other who was in England, live with their wives, and Sam Speare on the mainland opposite Zanzibar at Magila.

The native Christians at Kwamagwaza were much pleased at our introducing into our stained glass windows the three African subjects referred to. They were delighted to know that on the only occasions upon which Africans are spoken of in Holy Scripture they are represented as being engaged in good works.

St. Mary's, Zululand, October 29, 1872.
We are so comfortable now with our native girls: three big ones, a little one, and a married woman form our establishment; so willing, cheerful, and obedient, E. says he would not exchange them for English servants. And it is quite beautiful to see how well they agree among themselves; we never by any chance hear them squabbling.

Our old King Panda is dead; he died a week ago, we believe, but it is the custom to say the king is very sick, is in a fainting state, until he is buried, and then they announce it publicly; but until that time orders are given as usual in his name. The Zulu kings are left in their huts until the flesh has corrupted and the bones are white. They then bury them in their hut, and set a guard for a year or so to see that the people do not steal their *hair* or *nails*, these being considered powerful weapons against their enemies. I expect there will be a great hubbub, and I am afraid much war. Some say that the English will side with Cetewayo, some say they will help his brothers who are in the colony.

And now I must tell you about a robbery committed upon us. E. had a very handsome war shield and three spears, which he was going to send home. These hung in the verandah close by my bedroom door. Five mornings ago they were stolen, together with some nice skins we had nailed on to the chairs. We did not discover the loss until the evening. We were quite miserable, being afraid some of our boys had done this, for we felt quite sure a raw Zulu would be afraid to do it. Next morning two of our men (heathen) came for their wages, saying they must go home. This looked suspicious, so we were just arranging with Martyn that he should follow on horseback, and search their bundles, when two Zulus came running in to E. begging him to go to a wounded man at once.

A madman, they said, had in some way or other got hold of some spears, *where* they could not tell, for they always kept their own out of his way, and he had rushed after a young fellow who was milking in the *kraal*, and had stabbed him in the abdomen. We went off at once, and found that it was indeed the madman who had come into our verandah and taken these things, together with a volume of Keightley's *History of Rome* and some of Edie's clothes which were on the line behind the house, and a *beer-bottle*. But the most wonderful part of the story is this: the spear went in at the abdomen and came out just above the left hip, and the young man drew it out *himself* and flung it at the madman, and I am most thankful to say killed him. It was a horrible spear to be wounded with, being barbed. It was an awful wound, the bowels having protruded. E. sewed up one wound, leaving the other open, and keeping it dressed with arnica and water. This is the fourth day, and he is still alive, but inflammation of the bowels is what we are afraid of. E. goes morning and evening, and this evening thought his voice a little stronger.

Sunday, November 3.—Our patient is, I hope, progressing. We visit him three times a day to dress his wounds, and see that he takes his medicine, for the Zulus are either so wilful or careless, that unless we put the medicine in their mouths ourselves, after the first day they get tired and leave off. We cannot but be thankful that the madman did not attempt to enter the house, or that E. did not hear him; for if he had, and had gone out, he might have had a spear flung at him. I am not sure of this, for the black man has a great awe of the white man, and looks upon him as a very superior being, but I don't quite like to think that I had only a glass door between me and the madman. I have always been rather afraid of this man, and am very thankful that he is dead.

Our verandah just now is quite like a conservatory. E. has filled up one end with trellis-work, and has trained roses and honeysuckles up, and the scent of them is most exquisite. Do you know that beautiful white French honeysuckle?

We are hoping and hoping that Bishop Tozer may come down to see us. We heard from Miss Tozer the other day: she said her brother had quite broken down again, and she wished she could send him to us; but the difficulty was the getting here, there being no direct communication.

November 9.—Still no post; so we must send forty miles again, to Rorke's Drift, to save the mail. If you do not hear by next mail do not be alarmed, for E. says he cannot continue to do this.

I will send you a few mealies in time to sow. Dibble them in about two inches apart; they like plenty of manure, and water at night. They would look handsome down each side of a path. They grow twelve feet high. If you are sheltered you might sow at the time of spring wheat sowing.

Little Edie can now say everything, and often carries on a long conversation—of course in Zulu. It is so pretty to see her love for her Zulu nurse. I offended the old nurse the other day. The child had broken ten of her hen's eggs, and I wanted to replace them. She said, "Are you going to pay me for what my own child has done? My things are my child's."

We were talking the other day about our advantages and disadvantages. One comfort we have is this—we never have to think of the kitchen dinner. The girls have a large pot of porridge in the morning, and another in the evening. "*Kupela*"—"that is all." Sometimes there is no meal, but they do not say anything till dinner-time, when, if I have not found it out before, they will say, "*Silambile*"—"we are hungry."

It will be remembered that the servant girls gave Mrs. Wilkinson much trouble at first. She called them 'the plague of her life.' This was when she could not speak to them, and had not learnt their ways. An improvement was soon apparent, and her excellent management and sweet disposition attached these girls warmly to her. The foregoing letter testifies to their excellent conduct, and they are represented as being 'willing, cheerful, and obedient.' There could not be a character more admirably suited to manage the Zulus than hers. She could do *anything* with them. They are like animals, and watch you as closely as animals, and seem to know by a kind of instinct whom to obey and serve, and whom to disobey and despise.

St. Mary's, Zululand, Dec. 4, 1872.

We have been in dreadfully low spirits, having been two months without any news from the outer world; for the rivers have been so flooded and the country so disturbed, that the Natal *kafirs* were afraid to come into Zululand. It is a fact, which you will hardly credit, that in Natal they have quite as misty and fearful ideas of Zululand as anyone in England. The fact is, that Natal *kafirs* have been so often trading and stealing Zulu cattle, and, at the same time helping boys and girls to run away across the Tugela to the colony to such an extent, that Cetewayo has given orders that all Natal *kafirs* travelling without a white man are to be seized and beaten, and their cattle taken from them;

but that all *kafirs* travelling with the missionaries' letters are to be respected. This, on the other side of the Tugela, has been construed into, "every Natal *kafir* is to be killed." So our postmen were afraid to come.

We are having a most horribly wet time, four days wet and one and a half fine, then wet again. E. talks of sending a man to see if there is any water left in the Indian Ocean. I often think how A. would delight in this beautiful air; I mean, of course, when it is fine weather—always the same rare air which you feel on a mountain top. One of the most beautiful sights on a fine summer morning is to see the clouds lying like a lovely lake over the Umhlatuzi valley, which is about fifteen miles off; and on a clear day to see the sea so perfectly that one feels quite sure if a steamer were to pass one must see its smoke. Though it is very hot sometimes, I have suffered from heat much more at home than I have ever done here.

I have just returned from a strange work. A beast has just been shot, and I have been superintending the cutting up and salting, to give away to our poor famishing people. You would look on and wonder at all the things I have learnt to do since I have been here, I often think how *practically ignorant*, if you know what I mean, one is at home, and how clever one would appear there now, and up to emergencies. Here, if you do not exercise your wits you have to go without many things, and truly experience is a good teacher.

I am hoping that the new Metropolitan, whoever he may be, will be consecrated at Capetown, and then I shall do my best to make E. go, and shall go and stay with Mrs. Macrorie with the bairns.

A panther, or a leopard, has been committing ravages Amongst our sheep. First it took six, then twenty. Then we folded the sheep in the cattle *kraal*. We poisoned the dead meat, but cannot kill them.

Thus ended the year 1872—chiefly occupied, except during the journey to Amaswaziland, in steady hard work upon the mission station in Zululand. The next year, as will be seen, found Mrs. Wilkinson performing long and very fatiguing journeys, through which much new and valuable work was opened out. Those journeys laid many and very real hardships upon her, but she made no trouble of them.

I have seen her lay herself down to rest night after night wrapped in her blanket, her side saddle for her pillow, either on the earth floors of Zulu huts, or in decayed sheds, where an English farmer would not put his calves. And this with as thankful and contented a heart as if in a comfortable English home. A word of complaint was a very rare word with her; all was done lovingly and cheerfully for His sake, whose work she did, as she did every other work which her hand found to do, *with all her might*.[1] Her letters on this account now became less regular and frequent than when in settled life upon the station.

St Mary's, Zululand, March 5, 1873.

I must tell you about our dear Putu. God has been very merciful to us in answering our prayers. She is much better, although still only a poor little skeleton. One afternoon we thought she could not live through the evening. She lay in my arms with her mouth open, eyes half shut, and showing only the whites of her eyes. Her breathing was very laboured. E. was on the point of sending for Mr. Samuelson to come up to bury her, but something, he said, seemed to keep him back. I am so thankful that we never once felt, "Oh, that we had a doctor." We never once wanted anything which we had not by us.

Miss R. and I have not had our clothes off for ten nights. I am

---

1. In those parts of the country infested by lions, leopards, and panthers, the natives always billet a certain number of goats and calves upon each hut in the *kraal* for the night, for the sake of protection. Visitors are not exempt from this; we had, therefore, at times to share our hut with these creatures. They would remain fairly quiet during the dark hours, huddled together as far from us as they could well get in a small circular dwellings not five yards across. With the first streak of dawn, however, they would come and look into our faces and blare into our ears, and become such an abominable nuisance that we used to unfasten the little wicker door, which closes the entrance hole to a Zulu hut, and drive them out double quick.

Mrs. Wilkinson, after a while, resisted this custom. When she reached a *kraal* at night and was selecting a hut she used to say, 'Now, no calves and goats, remember; English people don't like sleeping with such, companions.' This used to cause great merriment. 'Do you hear!' they used to say, 'the white chieftainess says she does not like to sleep with our calves and goats;' and she generally got her way.

I have frequently known her succeed in winning over the Zulus when we had entirely failed to do so. In the matter of food, for instance, in scarce seasons. We would go round from hut to hut and beg a few mealies or beans or an *ucamba* of milk, but all in vain. 'Let me try,' she would say, and creeping out of the hut, we would soon hear her arguing and bargaining with the women and girls, which invariably ended in a triumphant return with a bevy of pretty Zulu girls at her heels, in fits of laughter, with an abundant supply of food on their heads.

sure she would have died without Liebig's Extract of Meat. For days her extremities were cold and clammy. E. says he never will again despair while there is life. It was very hard work nursing her, for she refused to leave me. She never slept more than half an hour at a time. Little Edie eats a great deal of a Zulu food called "*amasi.*" It is milk quite thick. We cannot touch it—it tastes so sour; but it is not really sour, and the *kafirs* boil mealies and grind them and mix it. No wonder the child is so strong, she is in the air from morning to night.

Tell F. we have just broken in our filly. He will laugh at the simple process. Martyn, who is very quiet and patient, put on a halter, and made her run round and round till she was tired and quiet. Then we put on a bridle and repeated the running. After that he put on a saddle, and repeated the process. Then one of the boys got on her back, she standing as quiet as possible. Martyn mounted another horse, and with a leading rein they cantered away. The next day Martyn saddled and bridled her in the stable, and mounted her himself, another man also going with him on the horse.

The next day E. himself mounted her. She went so nicely, though of course not accustomed to obey the rein, but E. managed her well; and now she is, I might say, broken in. The other day, however, E. had several battles with her; but when you think that she has only been ridden five times altogether, that is not wonderful. I have not mounted her yet, but horses out here do not mind the habit. My saddle has had hard work, and rough work too, having served as pillow and umbrella very often.

Tell F. my beet and cabbages are doing very well, and my mealie gardens are splendid. I get women to hoe them for about 3*s.* per acre. The mealie is a fine plant; it grows here seven feet high, and has two ears of corn as we might say, wrapped up in a number of green sheaths, with a lovely tuft of silky fibres growing out at the top. In good land they will yield about sixteen *coombs* to the acre. We are now in the midst of our peach crop. We have bushels, and we throw lots to the pigs. But you must not think they are like English peaches, they are much smaller and harder, Down in the Umhlatuzi valley, only ten miles off, every tropical thing will grow, but I would not live down there on any account, I would rather have this cold poor soil than the hot rich valley.

The account given above of the little child's dangerous illness is given in full, because it is well that those who have never lived far away in a savage country, where no medical aid can be obtained in times of sickness, should know how anxious a missionary's life is at such times. It may prepare some for such a life, and make others, who have no intention of entering upon it, more considerate towards, and more willing to help missionaries in their arduous duties and many trials.

St. Mary's, Zululand, March 16, 1873.

People all round Zululand seem to be in a great fright about war. The Dutch are trying to claim half Zululand, and naturally enough the king, Cetewayo, does not like it, and refuses to let it go. About us in Zululand things are very quiet. Cetewayo has just sent for Mr, Shepstone, the Secretary in the colony for native affairs, to come and make him king. So long as the English are his friends I do not think we need fear the Dutch. I tell you all this, for you may hear rumours, and think that we are hiding such things from you. The Norwegian missionaries are again in disgrace.

One of them reported the old king's death, which is quite against Zulu etiquette. He is not supposed to be dead until his successor is made king, and one of them interfered about the gun trade, which Cetewayo did not at all like. E.'s rule is, have nothing whatever to do with politics, either in or out of the country, but keep to your own work. We are *far safer* here than in Natal, where there are housebreakings, murders, &c. Here such things are unknown, the black man not having been taught the vices of the white man; consequently, he holds us in great respect, that is, if he sees that we keep him in his proper place. We always make them treat us as they do their great chiefs.

This was a very disturbed time indeed in and around Zululand. The king's death and the disunited state of his sons, with no assured succession, made Cetewayo's position exceedingly insecure, and ours no doubt to some extent critical.

As is well known, Mr. (now Sir Theophilus) Shepstone went into Zululand at Cetewayo's request, and crowned him king. This he did, exacting certain conditions from him, which Cetewayo when crowned *steadily and dishonourably refused to fulfil*. From the day of his coronation, under the aegis of the British Government, to the day our troops entered his country, his attitude towards us was one of broken faith, marked disrespect, and increasing insolence.

St. Mary's, Zululand, April 10, 1873.

You must indeed be careful, for rheumatic fever always leaves a person so delicate. You ask if this is a rheumatic place. When we came here the governor of Natal told us that those who were rheumatic in England did not suffer from it here, and *vice versâ*. He has proved right in E.'s case, for he used to have rheumatism at home, but never has it here. Indeed, I believe this to be a most healthy place.

How we should welcome you! I think a sea voyage would do you good. Suppose you come by the new route *via* Italy, Brindisi, Suez Canal, and Zanzibar. It has only been opened this year, but the changes of scene you would revel in. It is twenty-six days from Durban to Brindisi, and you would have a couple of days at Zanzibar, where you would change your steamer. Leave home next October. We are having now beautiful autumn weather. This afternoon we had a slight thunderstorm, but this evening it is delicious—almost a frosty air—with the beautiful Paschal moon shining so clear and bright, that one could read small print easily by its light.

E. baptized two young people last Sunday—a lad of about eighteen, and a young woman of about twenty, and he is going to confirm two young men on Sunday. One is from Mr. Samuelson's station.

As soon as the Robertsons come home, we hope to start for New Scotland. I shall go in the waggon with the children, and native boys and girls. E. will ride with Mr. Carlson round by the Bombo, a mountain range that divides Amaswaziland from Amatongaland. He will try to find a suitable place on this range, which is quite healthy, on which to settle Mr. Carlson, and from whence he can reach the Amatonga. He also hopes to place out this year Martyn and William Heber. He will try them for a year before he ordains them. John Fea, the other candidate, has drawn back from the work.

Jolin Fea fell about this time under the influence of a trader, who did him no good. Traders too often not only hinder Mission work by their own bad examples, but prevent those who would themselves engage in it by speaking against the work, and discouraging it by every means in their power. John Fea having a weaker mind than the other two fell away, under this bad influence, from his good purpose, and abandoned the idea which he took up readily at the first, and for the carrying out of which he promised well. He has since lost his wife, a nice creature, and it may be hoped that this sorrow may bring him back again to his good purpose.

St. Mary's, Zululand, April 26, 1873.

Our hands just now are very full of doctoring. One man has been here nearly a month with the most awful finger you can imagine. He was fighting, and was bitten by another man. At the end of ten days he came to us. His whole hand was terribly swollen. It has been a horrid thing to dress, but now a great piece of bone has come away, and it is healing up. Another man is here with a bad heel from a gunshot wound, which has been badly healed. We really are getting to know a little about doctoring, simply through practice. Never a day passes but at least three or four come for medicines, and medicines are very expensive out here. A small bottle of a certain kind of medicine,—of which we use much for a very common complaint amongst the Zulus (*entozoa*)—costs 21*s*. The man who was stabbed, and whom E. *sewed up*, is quite well.

Our garden now is so pretty—full of roses, heliotrope, and geranium. Our terraces are all edged with rose hedges of different kinds, which E. keeps well clipped. You will be sorry to hear that we have sickness amongst our cattle again, and they are dying fast. We have cured two or three by giving them about two handfuls of salt and two square inches of soap in a quart of water. This is a very strong medicine, and either kills or cures.

Little Edith always calls me "*Inkosikazi*," "chieftainess." The other day she frightened Mr. Carlson out of his wits. He was on the scaffolding working at the church, and she suddenly appeared at the top of the ladder, which has fifteen staves, and called out "*buka mina*," "Look at me." He dared not move lest he should frighten her. So he said quietly, "Go down, Edie," and she went down quite safely. Our church is now roofed in, and we are finishing the gables. All the windows also are in.

The people here grow tobacco in great quantities. I bought forty pounds the other day for 4*s*. It is not manufactured, I mean thread-like. It is in great rolls, like huge cigars, of eighteen pounds weight. I am very found of buying. I bought a quantity of tobacco two years ago. Everyone laughed at me, and wanted to know what I was going to do with it, and E. laughed most of all. But the next year came a famine of tobacco, and the people can go without food sooner than snuff, so E. had to come down from his laughing, and was very glad of it to give away, for our poor people had neither snuff nor food.

We shall see such splendid herds of game when we go up to New Scotland—*hartbeests*, zebras, gnus, ostriches, and all kinds of antelopes; I hope we shall shoot some. Gnus are something between a buffalo and a horse. *Hartbeests* are between a deer and a horse. They come down from the colder regions in search of grass, for the further north you go in winter the less rain you have.

The enormous herds of blesbok, springbok, gnu, and *quagga* (or zebra) which we used to see on those horseback journeys on the high *veldt* of the Transvaal were *marvellous*. We once found ourselves beyond Langs Nek, in the midst of one of these vast herds, which were trooping down from the tablelands of the Drakensberg, an altitude of 6,000 to 7,000 feet, to the lower *veldts*. They do this, in order to escape the cold of the higher regions, and the snow which falls in considerable quantities in the region of the source of the Vaal River, in the neighbourhood of Heidelberg. We had been sleeping the night upon one occasion at a Dutchman's farm—old Standers, of Standers Drift, on the Vaal River. His house is situated on a large plain, under a little rocky *kopje*. When we left this house early in the morning, a mist enshrouded us. As it lifted, the whole plain, as far as the eye could reach, was *one moving mass* of blesbok, springbok, gnu, and zebra.

We were in the midst of one of the great herds. Hundreds of thousands, and thousands of thousands beyond number, were on that plain and all around us that morning. We never saw such a sight before, and never did again. Although the plain had not a bush upon it, these herds made it look like a dense bush-*veldt*. Each kind of animal moved in its own herd without intermixing. As the springbok came to the waggon track, they would bound gracefully up into the air and clear it. When several dozens are thus in the air at the same time in one company, they look like a bridge spanning the waggon track. We also, upon this same occasion, saw vast swarms of locusts.

Upon one occasion, we rode for three days through a swarm. They

121

move *with*, and cannot go *against*, the breeze. The air was filled with them, like flakes of snow in a dense snowstorm. They obscured the sun; they covered the grass till it was brown instead of green. Wherever they appear the farmers light fires round their young corn, and send out the natives with pots and pans, pokers and fire-irons, to make as much noise as possible, with a view to keep them up in the air, that they may pass over the precious crop. If once they alight no fires, pots, pans, pokers, or fire-irons in the world can avail to get them up again till the crop is even with the ground.

The country may be as the Garden of Eden before them, but behind them they leave nothing but a desolate wilderness. The same may be said of the herds of wild animals, above described. They crop all the young grass to its roots, and foul every spring and stream of water which may come in their way. If the locusts are carried out to sea by the wind they fall on to the waves and perish. The coast of Natal has been covered two feet thick with their dead bodies, confirming what we read of their destruction in Egypt, when the strong west wind carried them away into the Red Sea and destroyed them.

St. Mary's, Zululand, April 1873.

All our poor neighbours are in such distress. A short time back, a nice old man close to us was accused of bewitching the cattle, and causing the Bush sickness, which I think I told you was bad about here. He fled away, and his sons remained about with the neighbours. At last orders came from Cetewayo that the sons were to be killed as well, one a great favourite of ours. They fled away also. Cetewayo, in his anger, has taken away every single beast from all his tribe, and it is a very large one, situated all around us. Two men have been killed, because they sheltered the sons for a time, and their poor wives and children have run to us, their houses being scattered, fourteen in number.

One young man has a spear wound in his shoulder, but, thanks to arnica, and his coming to us at once, it is doing beautifully. Generally, when they get wounds they try to cure them themselves, and when they are much inflamed, and a quantity of matter has accumulated, they come to us; and often it is discouraging to have such cases to deal with.

We are starting for Amaswaziland and the Transvaal. I shall have ridden a good 800 miles,[2] before I get back. We have the chil-

---

2. The 800 miles ride turned out to be 1,200 before it was finished.

dren under the care of Elizabeth, the old Zulu nurse. We were going to start today, but we heard yesterday that Mr. Shepstone is coming up to place Cetewayo on his throne, and is coming to us, so E. wishes to be at home to receive him. I hate this delay, because I had made all my arrangements, and now I shall have to make them over again. It may now be three weeks or so before we go. We had intended going in the waggon and taking the children, but we have had such cold nights that we thought it would not be safe to expose them to the cold. You have no idea what a steady, thoughtful person Elizabeth is. She is so fond of Putu, her pet name for baby.

CHAPTER 10

In the Transvaal, and On the Bombo

Pretoria, Transvaal, Aug. 20, 1873.

You will be amazed at the above address, so I think I cannot do better than give you an account of our adventures, from the time of our leaving home on Monday, July 21. E. and I, accompanied by the faithful Martyn, started on horseback. When we had ridden about two hours Martyn discovered that he had dropped our sugar and coffee. So we stayed at a *kraal* whilst he went home for more. Thus we spent our first day. On the third day we arrived at a German Mission station, situated under a high mountain, with a waterfall at the back of the house, and across the plain, in front of his house, another beautiful mountain called Intaba 'Nkulu, *i.e.* "the great mountain." It rises straight out of a large plain. It is a beautiful place, and E. (I say) always shams sickness that he may stay here and lie on the grass, listening to the waterfall.

At this station we bought a very nice young horse, for we were obliged to leave my mare there.

On the Saturday, at sunset, we reached Mr. Jackson's, the young horse being quite done up; for he is only three years old, and we had ridden about ninety miles in the two days. We remained with Mr. Jackson at the Amaswazi station the following week, and on the Sunday E. baptized the first Swazi boy, a nice little fellow of about ten. He is Mr. Jackson's very own, having once been a little slave. Other Amaswazi lads there are most anxious to be baptized, but their friends are very much against it; and although they could do nothing to prevent it, Mr. Jackson being situated just outside Swaziland, he thought it wiser to wait a little, and conciliate the people, for he has only been amongst them two years. During the week we were engaged trying our horses and Mr. Jackson's in harness; for Mr. B., a settler here, promised to drive us to Pretoria in his Cape cart with four horses. They all pulled as if they had been accustomed to harness all their lives.

So on Monday morning Mr. B., E., and I started with six horses, driving two, intending to pick up a four-in-hand set of harness on the road, Martyn leading the others. The first night our misfortunes began. One of Mr. Jackson's horses died from eating too many mealies the night before. Yon should have seen the *house* in which we lodged that first night. Its owner was away, and the habitable part was locked up, but we rummaged about and found an old rick cloth which we laid on the floor of a room, to which I must tell you there was no window and no door only the bare framework, and a great hole in the roof. So you can imagine it was not very warm, considering we were almost on the top of the Drakensberg. However, in displacing the rick cloth we found seven eggs, and in a cupboard a ham and some coffee, so we—as a matter of course in this country—helped ourselves, and had an excellent supper.

The next day we arrived at the house where we were to borrow the harness, a Mr. Bell,[1] who has the management of large herds of cattle and sheep for the Glasgow company. We started merrily on the Wednesday, with our four horses—Kelly, our dear horse, and Alma (the little mare E. broke in five months ago) as leaders. Towards evening we reached a store, where we had some dinner. A thunderstorm coming on, we could go no farther, and in the night Kelly and Alma and a horse belonging to Mr. B. (one of the wheelers) strayed, and we have never seen them since. It was bitterly cold up there.

We had therefore only two horses left, the one Martyn was riding, and the other wheeler. Mr. B. was afraid to go on with these, as one had never been in harness. So there was nothing to be done but return with these two, which took us very well, however; and on the Saturday we got back to the Amaswazi station, having had a week's knocking about for nothing. But I have not told you of the game.

---

1. Mr. Bell, the magistrate at New Scotland. He was *assegaied* by the natives about two years ago, (as at time of first publication), in a fray about some natives who had squatted on his land.

We travelled over vast plains, quite flat, never in fact arriving at the horizon, most wearying to the eye; but at this time relieved by thousands and thousands of wilderbheest (gnu), blesbok, and springbok. The gnu is such a funny fellow, with a tail like a horse, and thick upright mane, and shoulders like a buffalo. We saw some zebras, which trotted before us for some time, and three ostriches; but these were not near enough to see their plumage. Here the traders pay the Dutch 10s. for every large feather. I never saw such a sight as the wild animals. Sometimes there would be a race to cross our road, then we would divide the herd, and it would try to cross again further on—our horses getting so excited at the scene.

We rested on the Sunday at the Amaswazi station, from which we had started, and then left again on the Monday morning to try another route,[2] hoping to catch a post cart to this place. When we arrived at Wakkerstrom, from whence it starts, we found it did not leave for five days. We could not wait, so we bought another horse, and half on wheels and half on horseback we at last reached Pretoria yesterday. We have had the advantage certainly of seeing the country. There is work waiting for E. at Potchefstrom, but we have no time to go there, as we must make haste home before the wet season sets in.

We have found many rough places amongst the Dutch, the lower class of whom are much dirtier than the Zulus. The night before we got to Pretoria we had to sleep in the kitchen of a Dutch farmhouse on an old piece of canvas, in company with a *kafir* and a Hottentot! But we always carry each our own blanket. We are now staying with the German Lutheran missionary. He has a nice church, and day and evening school. The latter is for the *kafirs* working in the town. E. went in last night, and saw eighty candidates for baptism. Was not that a cheering sight?

We arrived on Saturday night, about three hours' ride short of the town of Heidelberg. On Sunday morning a gentleman drove us in that E. might give them an evening service. When we arrived we found that one of the inhabitants had brought the Wesleyan minister from Pretoria for that purpose. The inhabitants are chiefly Presbyterian, but they are willing to receive an English clergyman, and E. is very anxious to get one to take two or three towns of the same size, and give them a monthly

---

2. A route which took us near Langs Nek.

or six-weekly service.

I am going to try and get a diamond and some Lydenburg gold, to send home to make a locket for E. I do not like this country so well as Zululand; one gets weary of these everlasting plains, and not a tree to be seen. We have now ridden nearly 600 miles.

The first Swazi boy, baptized upon the occasion of this visit, was named Harvey, after the Bishop of Carlisle, who had always taken a great interest in our mission. He was a slave taken in intertribal war, and given to Mr. Jackson. The font used for the baptism was a gourd hollowed out for the purpose. A very nice heathen Swazi family lived, at this time, near our Amaswazi station. Several pleasant, intelligent boys belonging to this family came and attached themselves to Mr. Jackson. The old father in his heart liked his boys to be with us, but to keep up appearances before the Amaswazi authorities, who were at that time opposed to our work,[3] he made now and then a raid upon the station, with a big stick, and chased the boys in and out the building with feigned threats of a thrashing, if they did not return; the end of the raid generally being the regaling of the old man, and his departure in peace. These were 'the other lads' referred to, 'most anxious to be baptized.' Dear, good fellows they were, willing and industrious, and we were very fond of them. In the following letter from Mr. Jackson they are frequently mentioned.

The lost horses were supposed to have been destroyed by lions, which infest that district. They were subsequently found, however, many miles away by a Bushman, and brought back by him. It was during this visit to the Transvaal that the inhabitants expressed everywhere a great desire that the English Church should be introduced amongst them, and led to the foundation of the see of Pretoria in 1878.

Reference has been made to Mr. Jackson's work in Amaswaziland, who, in conjunction with his coadjutor, Mr. Hales, has watched over that Mission from its commencement with a father's care. This work— now so eminently crowned with success, having gained the full favour and approval of the Amaswazi king—was always deeply interesting to Mrs. Wilkinson, who was in the habit of staying for some weeks every year at this station on the edge of Amaswaziland, and taking her share in the work. The two letters which follow will not, therefore, be out

---

3. Within the last few days I have heard from Mr. Jackson that the Swazi king has invited him to build two mission stations in his country.

of place, giving as they do much interesting detail and insight of that work, and the attempt made at this time to reach the Amatonga nation through the Bombo Mountains.

New Scotland, Amaswaziland, July 11, 1872. Here I am at Clifton House once more. I arrived on the 5th instant, after an absence (at the Bombo Mountains, Amatongaland) of thirty-one days, and having that morning walked eighteen miles before breakfast, I was thus able to sit down with my friend, Mr. Hales, and combine breakfast and dinner in one meal. The grass was so wet and the ground so very soft that, had I not been near home, I should probably have been tempted to stay at the *kraal* for another day. As I could not conveniently bring my waggon back at the time, I preferred leaving it there on the flat to come up with Mr. Bolt; and I myself came back on foot. My work was then finished, and to have stayed longer would have been only a waste of time. Besides, I was anxious to get at the books, &c., expected from Zululand. On my arrival, however, the boys had not arrived, but came the same evening. I wish you could have seen the little boys in their tunics: [4] how pleased they were, and how well they looked. Their sister, the same age as Umcitaza (twins), has been here during Utyoza's absence, and until today, when her mother told me she wanted her to help her at home for a time, as she has much work just now. She is a very nice girl, and has got on quickly in reading and writing. She seemed quite sorry when I told her she must go home; but her mother says she may come again when the work is finished. Their father likes them to come, and encourages them to do so. This is cheering, as it is so very different from what we usually expect. The little girl's name is Untoyake. Umciteka still gets on well, and is a good little fellow. I was talking with him the other day, and asked him, "*Inhliziyo yako itini na?*" Wapendula, "*Inhliziyo yami isikoliwe.*" "What says your heart?" He replied, "My heart is to be a Christian." He has the best Scripture knowledge, and answers readily.

Utyoza's time is up, but he still wishes to stay. He says, "*Wena wedwa u Umlunga wami, u Inkosi yami.*" "You alone are my white man, my chief." Umehloncili also is still in my employ. His time was up a few days ago, and he wished to go home to see his

---

4. These were the nice boys pursued with a stick by their father, as related previously.

friends. He has done so, and taken my cattle with him to herd them at his home, since it is a much warmer place than this. There has been snow here, and the large hill near Mr. Tozen's place has had snow on it for twelve days. The boys' message to the *Inkosikazi* (Mrs. Wilkinson) for their tunics is *"siyatokoza,"* "we rejoice."

You will probably have seen Titus,[5] one of the natives who were to come and thatch for you. David came here yesterday with two other boys (Christians), one of whom wanted to stay with me. He said he wanted very much to live with me, and did not care about much money if I would only take him, as he had taken a liking to me since he saw me at Mr. Meyer's station. Mr. Meyer, too, asks me to look after them, and keep them right as long as they may be near me. Titus would no doubt tell you that a Zulu *impi* has been to Mr. Meyer's station and killed some of the heathen there, and taken away a great quantity of cattle.

The two boys told me about Prince Umahanana and the three girls. I hope you had no particular difficulty, but we are anxious to hear. I must not forget to tell you how much the two boys wondered at all they saw at Kwamagwaza. The bell, which they heard the first night, seems to have struck their attention; then the trees; and again, the service. Utyoza's uncle told me the other day that Zululand seems to have turned his head, and he does not know what he means to do, but he can talk about nothing except what he saw at Kwamagwaza. I have hopes of several of these boys, and it seems God will always find us something to do. I mean, as I told you when here, to have much teaching; not much manual labour, and wages in proportion.

The few pictures are already in use, and I believe with good effect. Of boys I believe we shall have a good number ere long; girls will not be so easily obtained as I had hoped. I tried during my last journey, but the people are afraid of me. It will take some time for them to know me properly, and I must begin with the chiefs. Umagwazatile (the Prime Minister of Amaswaziland) came the day after you left us. We get on well together, and I hope he will be of service to me. But I wish we could have an introduction from the Natal Government. It seems so

---

5. Mr. Jackson's native catechist. News of the death of this excellent man has just been received, (as at time of first publication). He died on the Bombo mountain station, the first missionary to the Amatonga.

important, that I shall not take any decisive step until I know more definitely whether or not you are likely to succeed in that.

And now for the Bombo. You will have observed that from near the Drakensberg range to this place the country is level. From here to the Bombo flat the country is very broken. This latter distance is about sixty or seventy miles, and the road is rough and difficult to travel by waggon. The Bombo flat at the place where I crossed it is about forty miles across. This flat runs along the whole extent of the Bombo range, and is generally about thirty miles across. It has hardly any rises in it deserving the name of hill. Its character is what the natives call "*amhlanza*," *i.e.,* bush without underwood, such as you see about the Amatikula in Zululand, and other places along the coast.

It is very hot and unhealthy in summer. Even now in winter it is nearly as warm as it is here in summer. The water is bad, and few streams to be met with; we had to carry water with us. There is much game, and wild animals abound, such as lions, tigers,[6] wolves, and jackals. The elephant and rhinoceros also are seen in summer. Buffaloes, gnus, zebras, and deer (antelopes) go in troops. No natives live beyond a few miles from the edge of the flat.

The land here is good, and the bush not so thick as further on. Water, too, is more plentiful. There is not so much danger to be apprehended from lions. It is made much more unhealthy than it would otherwise be, by the numerous pools of stagnant water to be met with all over the flat. In winter they become dry, and so fever is not so prevalent as in summer. The fly also is found here, and this makes it impossible for cattle to be kept, except on the edge of the flat. The Bombo range stands up like a great wall about 800 feet above the flat, and seems as if it had buttresses of earth, in some places reaching about half-way up, and in other places nearly to the top.

There are few passes, and these difficult to climb; the natives, however, manage to get cattle up. Trees, such as are found on the flat, grow also on the side of the hill up to near the top. Almost immediately on reaching the top it is observed that the water flows to the east into the Amatonga country. The east side of the range is more broken, and descends gradually down to the

---

6. There are no tigers in Africa, but leopards and panthers are so called by Europeans.

Amatonga country, and is very much like the country between Mr. Oftebrö's station (Etyowe) and the coast in Zululand. The distance from the west to the east side cannot be more than three or four miles in some places.

The land there is good, and there is much wood in the *kloofs* and gullies for all purposes. As there is no sand on the hill, there might be some difficulty in getting good burnt bricks. Coffee would probably grow well, and I saw tobacco and sweet potatoes. A large amount of native labour could probably be obtained at a cheap rate, and sugar is grown in small quantities by the Amatonga, just under the mountain. I observed that some of the natives had to go a long distance for water, but this difficulty might be overcome by wells. The Amatonga would gladly come to work upon the mountain, and a person living there and choosing his time might, I believe, go down into the Amatonga country for days with impunity.

The greatest difficulties connected with the Bombo at present are these: (*1*) How to get goods there This can be done in two ways—1, By taking them this way (*via* Amaswazi station) in the winter time, and leaving the waggon at the last kraals on the flat, and then hiring bearers to take the goods forward; 2, By having the goods sent up from Durban to Delagoa Bay, and appointing an agent there to send them up the Usutu in a boat. There are, I understand, such agents in Delagoa Bay. (*2*) The complete isolation of the person stationed there. We, here, shall be his nearest white neighbours, and from this place to that is thirty hours' good walking, *i.e.* four days for a tolerably good walker. Communication might be had by means of native messengers, but it would not be convenient for white people to pass often. The place of which I am now speaking is the central position of the range, and the spot chosen by Mr. Mackorkindale for his intended road.

With respect to cattle, some said they do well there, but the people have not many; they are too poor. Another said they were afraid to keep them there, lest an enemy might cast longing eyes upon them. Others said they die some years, and live well in others. The cattle I saw there were in excellent condition; and the conclusion I formed is that anyone living there need never fear wanting milk and butter, and even a span of oxen might be kept for work upon the hills. A few pounds would make a road up the mountain on the Amatonga side, and donkeys might then be used for bringing goods up from the river.

I got on well with the chief, and he almost immediately offered to sell land. A judicious person might, I think, have a small tribe under him before long. But I think I have now said enough for once; it would take me a long time to tell you everything of interest connected with my journey. I picked up a good bit of information about the Amatonga and their country, but have not yet had time to put it on paper, and so must reserve it for another letter.

The story of the man Titus, who is spoken of in the earlier part of Mr. Jackson's letter, is an interesting one. Within sight of the Amaswazi station is a min. Some forty years ago a Mr. Alison, a missionary, came up to Amaswaziland, founded two stations, and began his work. Umswazi, the then king of Amaswaziland, heard that Mr. Alison was teaching the people of a King greater than himself. Umswazi said, 'This cannot be taught in my country, there is no king greater than myself.' He thereupon ordered the station to be destroyed, the native Christians to be killed, and the white missionaries to be driven away. The order was executed, Titus, then a boy, being one of those who escaped with his life.

After a lapse of some thirty years, Mr. Jackson made the second attempt to bring Christianity to the Amaswazi. He began to teach them at his New Scotland station, which was placed just over a hill in the immediate neighbourhood of the ruined station. He had not long settled there when a native presented himself, and said he should like to be associated in the work, stating that he was one of those who had escaped the slaughter in the reign of Umswazi. This was Titus, who has ever since been a faithful coadjutor to Mr. Jackson. Thus seed sprang from that ruin, and from that early work so terribly baptized in blood.

Mr. Jackson speaks of the caution he had to use in dealing with the people as a stranger in 1872, of their suspicion of him, and so forth. In a letter received from him during the Zulu war he speaks of their entire confidence in him; that while the Zulus had destroyed his property, the Amaswazi were not only protecting him, but were helping him at the risk of their own lives to gather in his harvest. He writes:

Since leaving my station on January 22, the day of the Isandhl-wana disaster, I have had no settled abode, but have been constantly moving about, and expecting that the Zulus might at any time make a raid into this part. We have, however, just lately come to settle on our land near to Derby. I have got up a grass hut, and am collecting building materials. Before very many days have passed I expect to commence brick-making, and shall get up a house as soon as possible.

A few days ago Hales and myself returned from our place at the Mahamba, where we made an effort to get away our mealies and other property not destroyed by the Zulus. I had a number of armed Swazies, given by the chief of the district, to accompany me, and help me to harvest my mealies, and carry away my broken tables, harmonium, and property worth carrying away. Whilst harvesting the Swazies had their guns close at hand, and many of them held an *assegai* under the left arm to be ready in case the Zulus should come down upon us suddenly.'

Here, then, were the Amaswazi, who refused to join the English against the Zulus for fear that the Zulus might conquer the English, and then overwhelm them for taking our side, standing by this lone missionary upon the dangerous border-land, and willing to lay down their lives, heathen as they were, at his side.

Mr. Hales also wrote a very interesting account of his journey to the Bombo under date—

New Scotland, Nov. 1, 1874.

You have, I believe, heard of my journey to the Bombo, and I will now try to give you some account of it. On Tuesday morning, September 26, at about half-past nine, in a thick mist and rain I made a start. At the end of about twelve miles I reached the first *kraal*; the people were smelting iron from stones, and making it into picks. A large stone set into the ground acted the part of an anvil; four or five large stones the sledge hammer, and a piece of iron, three inches long and two wide and about one inch thick, acted the part of a small hammer. The files and rasps with which they cut iron are different kinds of stone. The bellows consist of two bags sewed together on all sides except one corner, which is left unsewn, furnished with an earthenware nose for the wind to escape by. The top part is laced like a boot, so as to admit the wind.

This, I think, is only to keep them together, as they open at the top three or four inches. These rest on the ground, and as the blower lifts them up he opens them at the top, and closes them as they go down, and so forces the wind out of the bellows into another large pipe made tapering at the large end for the two pipes to enter to receive the wind, and convey it to the fire. This large pipe is placed just under the surface of the ground, so as to get the fire into a little hole, that it may be kept together. I think the whole of this process took about twelve persons.

I then moved off, as I had another six miles to do, and the sun was nearly down. I arrived at the *kraal* where I intended to sleep, and got a hut with a little trouble, but no food.[7] I felt hungry as I laid on my mat, but it could not be helped, so I made the best of it by hoping to get food in the morning at a great chief's, Umtyenga by name. I got to his *kraal* in about an hour, but only to be disappointed; for he had not got any food, or I should have got some from him. So we lost no time, but made the best of it, full of hope as before. About noon we arrived at a small *kraal*, at which I saw a few people burning a wooden dish to blacken it. I was dreadfully hungry then.

It seemed useless to try to buy food, as they always refused, so I tried another scheme. I came up to where they were sitting, and my native lad and I sat down to talk, &c. After a few seconds I made a horrid grimace, laid back, and shut my eyes. I then heard them ask my lad, Umcele, what I was doing. The boy, not knowing, but fancying that I was hungry, said, "Oh! do you not see that he wants some food?" Almostly instantly I heard one of them move away to get me some, but I still laid in the same posture. Presently the head of the village came with an *ucamba* of native beer. Umcele called me, and I got up in a slow manner and drank with Umcele, and felt much stronger and better. I am very glad that my plan answered so well, or I do not know what we should have done, the *kraals* being so far apart.

After leaving there we walked a long distance, and ;stayed at the next *kraal*. Here there was a boy about fourteen years old, who wanted to come back with me when I returned. I went and asked his brothers if he might do so, and after a time they agreed—mother, brothers, &c.—that he should return with me as I passed. When I returned I called for him, but they said he must herd the goats, so I lost him. A nice boy, I assure you, and one anxious to learn, and also to become a Christian. If the

7. It was a time of famine.

wish be real it will not die away but grow stronger. At the *kraal* where we slept in the evening some girls came in to talk while I was singing the hymn, "*Kwezikude izintaba*" ("Before the hills in order stood"). They sat down to listen, as the boy said quietly that I was singing. They tried to repeat the words after me, as I gave them distinctly. When I had finished they asked me to sing it again. I sang it three times, and then asked them to get me some food. They got it willingly, and cooked it.

Before the sun rose we set off. We had close upon forty miles to get over that day upon a cup of coffee and two cups full of boiled mealies. About half-way across the flat we came to the course of a river, but it was dry. The boy found a little water in a large stone to moisten our parched throats. This was the last water until we reached the top of the Bombo. After resting half an hour we started again, and when the sun was getting low found ourselves at the foot of the range. There was but one thing to do—to die or climb it—for we could not have gone on much longer. I could scarcely breathe, and the boy, Umcele, was the same. Some of the *kafirs* on the flat said, "That white man will die if he attempts to climb the Bombo." However, we got to the top, and a nice breeze refreshed us.

The next day I went to see the queen and her son, the young king Umbikisa. She was very nice, and so glad to see me, as one of her subjects is staying with us at our station. He is an elderly man, Umahou by name, who is recovering from an illness which none of the native doctors can cure. I liked the Bombo very well. It m quiet, and I think that in a few years a good and great work might be done. It is a difficult place to get at, everything having to be carried up on *kafirs'* heads. Should any one go there he must live hard and work hard, and be of a cheerful disposition. I think that one could live on the Bombo and descend to the Amatonga tribe at a certain season. The country is broken and stony on the top. They dig chiefly on the sides of these hills.

Mrs, Wilkinson's next letter was written on her way back from Pretoria.

Amaswazi Station, New Scotland, Sept. 6, 1873
We arrived back here the day before yesterday, after a long ride, which was very fatiguing, as our horses were very tired and

dreadfully thin. We found the mail letters waiting for us, brought up by Mr. Carlson from Zululand. Mr, Carlson brought sick news from home, everyone having been ill with measles and whooping cough, I am most anxious to get home. E. has gone with Mr. Carlson to the Bombo mountains. Martyn only arrived last night, his horse was too tired to come on quickly with us from Pretoria, If I can get a horse for Martyn I shall set off for Zululand with him alone.

We enjoyed our visit to Pretoria very much; everyone was so kind and hospitable—we were always lunching or dining out. They begged E. to help them, so he has consented to spend three or four months in every year with them. He bought a nice house and garden, almost the best in the place. The garden is full of fruit trees, oranges, &c. It will be a pleasant change every year, and I hope little Edie will learn to speak English there. The Pretoria people got up a *conversazione* for us—about sixty people were present. There was a succession of good singing and playing, not formal like a concert, but one could move about and talk to friends all the time. We were quite astonished; we had no idea Pretoria was such a pleasant place.

There has been no fighting in Zululand. The chief enemy to Cetewayo *died*, most opportunely! So the coronation was delayed a little time, whilst they *mourned* for him. He was an old man, Panda's Prime Minister, and a great enemy to Christianity; not that I think Cetewayo much better. E. is bemoaning the time when Martyn will be ordained, and can no longer be taken on these journeys.

You will rejoice to hear that we have found our horses. That wicked old Kelly is so fat with his holiday, the lazy old thing. I'll make him go when I get on his back again. E. bought me such a nice horse, Hans by name; he is what they call a "salted" horse, which means that he has had horse sickness and has recovered, consequently he is very valuable. E. gave 15*l.*, a long price in this country, though we might have sold him in Pretoria for 35*l.*, as no horses live there which are not salted.

The other day, as we were riding along, we saw forty zebras in one herd. They were close to us, and further on we saw five. We also passed an ostrich farm. They keep them for the sale of their feathers, which they pluck every year. I should like much to have seen an ostrich's nest, but we have never come across one.

They lay about thirty-six eggs; the outsiders are not hatched, but remain as food for the young ones. One egg equals twenty-four hens' eggs. We passed through the lion country. In a garden we saw three skulls of lions that had been killed close by. We met a man who was still suffering from the attack of a lion. He was travelling alone with two horses.

At night he lay down in the open. He lighted a fire, knee-haltered his horses, and went to sleep. But it came on to rain, and put out his fire. A noise amongst the horses awoke him, and he saw a lion and lioness pulling down his horses. He had a pocket revolver. As he got up he saw the lion spring at him, so he flung himself against it, and by that means was not thrown down. The lion seized him by the left arm. He fired two shots, which must have had some effect, for the lion went off. His arm was fearfully crushed, and he was wounded in the neck by a claw. He managed to sling his arm, and then walked seventy-two miles, when he fell in with a waggon, which took him another thirty, to a place where he found a doctor. This was about eight months ago. The night we met him he had been driving a four-in-hand, and his wrist was very painful.

The lion *veldt* between Pretoria and Erstelling goldfields in the North Transvaal is a very dangerous district to travel over alone. I once performed the journey, but in company with eight traders' waggons. Every night before sundown the leader of the convoy called out all hands to make a stockade of mimosa trees and branches. Into this enclosure the eight spans of sixteen oxen were driven, and fires lighted around, which were fed by natives all night. We often heard the lions during the night chasing antelopes along the gullies, and in the morning not unfrequently saw their footmarks in the neighbourhood of our camp. Two Dutchmen were once driving through this district in a Cape cart.

One moonlight night they trekked on late, and were attacked by two lions, which pulled their horses down and killed them. Unable to escape from the cart, which was a hooded one, with an exit only in front, they sat till dawn, prisoners in the vehicle. Whenever they made any movement with a view to slip out, the lions, thinking they were going to be deprived of their prey, turned and snarled at them, and then went on with their feast.

The visit made to the Bombo mountains with Mr. Carlson was

with a view to purchase land there of a chief upon which to found a Mission station. The Bombo range—in form like a great wall about 300 miles in length—divides Amaswazi from Amatonga lands. The latter is a coast kingdom in the diocese of Zululand, about 300 miles long by 80 wide. It is a fever district, and fatal, at present, to the white man *during the rainy season of the year.* In 1870 nine white men went into that country to hunt elephants for ivory, and none of them came out again.

About forty years ago the first attempt was made to take Christianity to the Amatonga nation. A party of German missionaries from the Cape Colony came up through Amaswaziland to the western face of the Bombo range. They, took their waggon to pieces—the mountain range, in shape like a gigantic wall, being inaccessible to waggons— and carried it over piece by piece, putting it together again on the other side. The natives on the Bombo still tell the tale how their oxen all died from being bitten by the Tsetse fly, and how the whole party perished by fever. The second attempt was made about seventeen years ago, and again by German missionaries. They found the tribes, however, on the top of the Bombo in such a disorganised state through intertribal warfare, that they returned without effecting anything. We made the *third* attempt, and obtained a fine tract of land of Umtyelequana, the paramount chief of that particular part of the Bombo.

Upon this land we erected a small hut to claim possession. No man volunteering for work in such a remote district, the mission to the Amatonga has never been commenced.[8] Our hope was to establish two or more stations on the *top* of the Bombo, which is *healthy*, and so to draw the Amatonga up to work for us there. We should then train them at our stations, and send them back as teachers to their own people, visiting them during certain months in the middle of the dry reason, when the Amatonga country may be safely entered by Europeans. This, I trust, may yet be done when the Delagoa Bay bishopric is founded.

Old Umtyelequana knew nothing of missionaries, never having seen any before. He was much exercised as to the propriety of letting the white man come and settle in his country. He could give us no answer, he said, until he had consulted the spirits of his ancestors. This he would do on the following day; and the following day he disappeared early and did not return until late. Where had he been? Into the bush to meet the spirits of his ancestors. Well, what did they say?

8. A native catechist has since been sent to commence this work.

Oh, they were quite agreeable to our coming, and we were therefore welcome to come and build. When all was settled he seemed much satisfied; we heard him say to one of his people, 'now we shall not be troubled with wild pigs anymore; the white man will shoot them for us.' Poor 'Umtyelequana! such was his idea of the office and utility of a missionary. We stayed for a day or two with a fine old petty chief on the Bombo.[9] He has been down to Natal, and had worked for a settler near Maritzburg. He used to attend the *kafir* service there; and he told us that he delighted in it. 'My heart,' he said, 'soared up like a bird whilst the preacher spoke,' and he flattered upwards with his hand, imitating the motion of the skylark.

He was much pleased at the idea of a mission being established amongst his people. 'I shall keep to one wife,' he said, 'as the white man does.' Poor man! we had not left him long before his wife was bitten by a snake, and died. I often think of the last I saw of him, when he conducted us early on the morning of our departure from his *kraal* to the high rocky precipices down which we had to scramble. Upon these he perched himself like an eagle, watching us and shouting his directions to us till out of sight.

The Bombo flat is a waterless, hot, bushy region, thirty miles wide, which had to be traversed before we reached. Amaswaziland again. A Tsetse-fly district, too, it is,, which had to be crossed on foot, and upon which we used to suffer much from heat and thirst. We once crossed it at night for coolness sake, but the native guides do not like to do so; they say it is dangerous, and so it is, for the flat is fall of wild beasts, the best hunting-ground in. that part of South-East Africa.

When crossing this Bombo flat upon one occasion with Mr. Jackson, we had with us an excellent native lad named Philip. At certain seasons the flat is entirely without water the whole thirty miles, save where a friendly shower may gain a lodgement in the hollow of the rocks. To cross this flat necessitates a guide, and since for coolness sake it is desirable for Europeans to cross it in the night, a guide is not easily procured; for the Bombo flat has a bad name, and natives rarely cross it alone or unarmed, and never after nightfall.

It was under a heavy bribe, therefore, that upon this particular occasion I at last, and with much difficulty, persuaded a young native,, who lived on the edge of the flat and knew the district, to accompany

---

9. During this visit to the Bombo I saw the blue and also the lilac water-lily. The former, in a pool on the Bombo mountains; the latter, in a stream on the flat. I did not know of its existence before.

us. At first he scorned the idea of going at night. No one ever heard of such a thing, he said. No one but a white man would dream of attempting it. Were there not herds of buffalo in the bush? Did not the flat abound with lions and hyenas? and were there not lurking leopards, and panthers, and creatures that laid along the tree branches ready to spring down upon the unwary traveller? No! nothing would induce him to go.

A large bribe, however, brought him to reconsider the matter. Would we wait till the moon was up? Yes, we would. Well, then, he would go. So we waited till the moon was up: and then, gathering up a bunch of spears and placing one amongst them the blade of which was as big as a large roach, he bade us follow him.

At the last stream we crossed before entering upon the flat he filled a gourd with water, informing us, as he did so, that it was the last water we should probably see until we arrived At the Bombo mountains, which look like a long, blue, lofty wall, when seen across the flat from Amaswaziland. Instead of one moderate-sized gourd, which was all we had, we ought to have provided ourselves with three or four such. And so we soon found to our cost; for as the day broke and the sun began to burn down upon us, the water in the gourd, as with Hagar of old, was soon spent; and we thirsted over that scorched and scorching 'flat' as I never thirsted before, and devoutly hope shall never thirst again.

My lips swelled, and we reeled along weak and giddy with the parching drought. Had it not been for some wild fruit which we found under the trees on the waste I do not know how we should have existed. Here and there we saw the hard sunburnt mud which marked the site of some old rain pool, deeply pitted all over with the footprints of various wild beasts, prominent amongst which was the lion; such a great round paw! These last drops of muddy ooze we drank greedily through our pocket-handkerchiefs, as filters, by throwing them on the surface.

Towards the afternoon we met a native, who seemed wandering about with no object, and who seemed to us a suspicious character, bent upon no lawful undertaking. Thinking he might be a scout to some marauding gang of natives, I felt rather uneasy for the rest of the day. In answer to our inquiries he said that in front of us we should pass the stump of an old tree, the withered branches of which had probably led a little water into it from the last shower of the last wet season. Near the tree we should find a shell, with which we might dip the water out, such as it was.

As we approached the old stump, a heathen lad, who had accompanied us with Philip (a Christian lad from Mr. Jackson's station), rushed on in front, and, seizing the shell, drank greedily of the water. We only just arrived in time to drag him away, and save the remnant that was left. The 'water,' if such it could be called, smelt offensively as we drank it, and was about the colour and consistency of weak coffee. To us, however, in our exhausted condition, it was nectar. Here the Christian lad's disciplined character came out in sharp contrast with that of the heathen lad. Philip never attempted to take a drop of the water himself, but patiently baled it out with the shell into the gourd, and when the dregs became so thick that we rejected them, as no better than a mild liquid manure, he began to drink the black ooze, as though it were the most sparkling spring water. This we would not allow him to do, but poured him out instead a cup of that which we had secured in the gourd, as a reward for his manly self-denial.

Night overtook us whilst we were yet on the bushy flat, and before we had reached even the foot of the Bombo range. We had been lying down at short intervals all the afternoon, being scarcely able to walk for more than twenty minutes consecutively. We now felt ourselves utterly unable to climb the mountain, upon the top of which we could alone rest in safety, and where we should once again find *kafir* kraals. As the sun went down, Mr. Jackson, who had borne the burden and heat of that day much better than I had, was about half an hour in advance of me. Arrived not far from the foot of the mountain wall I could go no farther, and told Philip to spread my mat, as I intended to sleep there. What! here in the bush amongst the wild beasts, unarmed, and without fire? Yes, here, beasts or no beasts. I could not go another step. So Philip spread my mat, and I laid down: he spreading his own, and lying down by my side. In a short while Mr. Jackson's native lad returned and begged I would come on to where they had established themselves, as it was better if we were to sleep on the flat, that we should be together. Unwilling to expose myself and Philip to any unnecessary risk, I stumbled on, and stumbled up the first broken flank of the mountain wall, one of the weariest half-hours I ever travelled in my life, and at last joined Mr. Jackson. Here we laid down, and, tired out with the day's journey, soon fell asleep.

How long I slept I do not know, but I was awoke by Philip touching me gently, and saying, 'Listen, listen, chief! Listen to those lions down there.' And there, sure enough, was something worth listening to. It seemed as though two lions were fighting together over their prey about half a mile or so from us. I had often read in books of the roar of the lion making the forest shake, but never believed it till that night. They appeared to me to be at, or very near the spot where we had recently been lying, and I said to Philip, jokingly, 'They smell where we were lying, and are angry because they are cheated of their supper.' 'Oh, *Inkosi*,' he replied, '*ngiyasaba*' ('Oh, chief, I am afraid').

Mr. Jackson, thinking it unsafe to stay where we were, begged me to try and go on. Through complete prostration, I felt that night utterly careless of wild beasts, and, if alone, should certainly have remained where I was; thus roused, however, I crept on and up the mountain side, until, just as the day dawned, we reached the top. Here we found water in some hollow places upon the flat rocks. We drank eagerly of it, and then laid down and slept until the sun was far up in the heavens.

From the summit of this range we could see clearly the sandy hills on the shores of the Indian Ocean near Delagoa Bay. We could also trace the courses of the magnificent tidal rivers, which, coming out of the mountains of Amaswaziland, pass through the Bombo range, piercing it by what are called *poorts*, and winding their way sluggishly through Amatongaland, empty themselves into the Bay.

This Christian lad, Philip, was a great comfort to us upon our journey, and by his good example at the various *kraals* at which we stayed could not have failed to leave behind him good seed. Such a steady fellow as Philip, who never neglected his prayers night and morning— and whom I have often overheard saying prayer with the heathen boys at our Amaswazi station—would tell the heathen, with whom he came in contact as we journeyed, of our Mission stations, of our ways and doings, and would do his best to induce other boys to come and work for us, and thus bring them within the influence of station life. Thus, whether at home, or travelling with us in heathendom, a good native Christian is the best missionary we can have at our side to recommend to his brethren the Gospel of the kingdom of Christ.

It may not be out of place to give here an incident in Philip's life, which shows this good fellow's wish to draw his relations after him to Christianity. In fact, it illustrates the secret of all the bitter opposition to Christianity we experience in Africa. The people know well that if *one* of a family joins us, that one will not be content until he has drawn after him his whole family. Thus they would rather kill such an one, and so, as they imagine, crush the movement in the bud, than lose (as warriors and hunters) a whole family. I will reserve the incident in question to the beginning of another chapter.

CHAPTER 11

Incidents of Native Christians

It is a common saying amongst the missionaries in South Africa that our *good* native Christian families are the best missionaries we have. There can be no more living or potent epistle of commendation of the faith of Christ in a heathen land than the sight of a Christian father and mother bringing up their children well. The presence of a well-ordered white family in the midst of heathenism exercises doubtless an incalculable influence for good, but this is to a certain extent *expected* of Europeans by the heathen. 'Christianity,' they say, 'is the white man's custom; it comes easily to him to read and write, to believe in and to serve God; but these things are not for the black man, he cannot understand them.' When, however, they see their own people able to master these things and to live them in daily life, it acts at once as an answer to their objection that the white man's customs are not for them.

The native Christians upon our stations have each their tract of land, apportioned or lent to them, upon which they build their houses, and graze their cattle, and a part of which they cultivate. Each, in fact, is a little farmer, and each therefore employs a certain number of lads[1] to help him in the work of herding and cultivation, while the wife will generally find work within and around her house for one or more heathen girls. Imagine, then, the influence which a well-ordered home is sure to have upon such heathen boys and girls. The reading of Holy Scripture and of other good books, the morning and evening family prayer which our best Christians never omit, the grace before meals, the children going daily to the Mission school, the Sunday rest and services in the Mission church—who can tell the power of God

---

1. The middle-aged and elder men amongst the heathen rarely work; the married men never.

unto salvation in all these things? What opportunities for doing good among their heathen brothers and sisters do our Christians possess; how well employed they are by some, how sadly and injuriously neglected by others!

James Martyn, the Hottentot or Ilawu, so often mentioned in these letters, and his wife Elizabeth were, with their little daughter Malia, one of the most satisfactory of the native Christian families upon the Mission station of Kwamagwaza. He was an industrious man, and kept his house, garden, and land in good order. He always had several heathen lads under his care, assisting him upon his little farm. It was well known amongst us that Martyn's lads always did well. They generally came to us after a while, and asked to be prepared for baptism.

Amongst them came one who in due time, and after due instruction, was baptized with the name of Philip, the lad who accompanied us upon our journey to the Bombo mountains, as related at the end of the preceding chapter. He was a quiet and industrious fellow, and though not brilliant, was nevertheless plodding and persevering. He found some difficulty at first in learning to read and write, but was always diligent and painstaking. In 1871 I prepared him for confirmation, but discovering that he smoked the '*insangu*' or hemp, I told him that I must adhere to my rule, and could not allow him to be confirmed unless he promised to give it up.

A great struggle went on in his mind; for it is very difficult to give up the habit. Several of our lukewarm Christians went back from Holy Communion on this account after I made the rule in question. Philip was, I believe, afraid to promise lest he should not be able to keep his promise. I reasoned and argued with him, but all apparently to no purpose. At last I said, 'Philip, you know much about Holy Communion, for I have long instructed you upon the subject; you know what a help it will be to keep you from old heathen ways. Do you really mean to tell me that you love that injurious "*insangu*" more than the Body and Blood of your Lord?' He hung his head a few moments, and then lifting it looked at me and said in Zulu, 'I will leave it off altogether.' And I believe he faithfully kept that promise. He was confirmed, and became one of the most regular and earnest of our communicants.

So satisfactory in every way did this young man's life become under the good home influence of Martyn's household, that in the year 1872 I asked Martyn to spare him from his work for half the day, in order that he might join the class of young men whom I was training for Holy Orders. Here he showed much promise, and made much progress, not only in scholarship, but in earnestness of purpose and anxiety to learn.

About this time Philip's life was nearly brought to an untimely end through an act which, in its motive comendable, and much to his credit, lacked that caution and judgement which so few young hot-blooded Zulus possess. At his *kraal*, some twenty miles distant, lived a favourite sister, whom he was most anxious should become a Christian. As I have already said, our best Christians will not rest until they have done all in their power to bring their heathen relations and friends under our influence. So it was with Philip; and in this case he endeavoured, in the spirit of St. Andrew, to win to Christ his own sister. We knew nothing of the plan which I am about to disclose; it was undertaken entirely at his own instance and upon his own responsibility. He arranged on a certain night to meet this sister in a reed bed beneath his *kraal*, and to fly with her to our station.

On the appointed night he was ready at the appointed place. The girl, however, knew that the attempt would be hazardous, and might even cost her life. At the last moment her heart failed her, for what reason I never learnt, and she discovered the plan to her people. I suppose she warned her brother to escape before divulging her intention, for, though the men of the *kraal* pursued him back to our station, he fled before them all night. Arrived at Kwamagwaza, they surrounded Martyn's house, where Philip, had taken refuge, and, armed with spears, demanded that he should be brought out and put to death.

I was absent from the station at the time upon a visit to Cetewayo. It was well for Philip perhaps that I was. Messengers were sent to us quickly, and arrived at the royal *kraal* whilst we were holding an interview with the king. The messengers were brought into the king's hut, and delivered their report of the affair. It was an opportune moment, for Cetewayo was—which was rarely the case—in a good humour, and when we pleaded for Philip he readily granted him pardon; and we promised to caution the lad; for such an act of indiscretion, said Cetewayo, must not be repeated.

Philip was at one time a frequent companion of mine upon my journeys in the north, and I always found him a most faithful and good fellow. His influence in the heathen *kraals* at which we stayed was always good. It is by no means always the case that our native Christian lads behave well when staying with us in *heathen kraals*, I am sorry to say. There are so many temptations in heathen life placed before these poor fellows at such times that it would be almost more than we could expect if they *never* fell under them. What we know to be deadly sins, they have been brought up to look upon as no sin at all. I remember once talking most seriously to a group of young heathen Zulus upon such sins; they listened to the end, and then looked up at me with the merriest faces and beaming eyes, and said, 'We cannot understand you, we see nothing wrong in all this.'

Philip, however, I could always trust. As we tarried here and there upon our way he would gather the heathen lads together in the evening over the hut fire where he was quartered, and tell them the story of our station life, and of those things which he had learnt amongst us. God only knows what good seed such a young man sows in such a dark land. He never went to rest at night or rose in the morning without prayer. If other of our Christian boys were with us I used to hear Philip conducting the morning and evening prayer with them from his Zulu prayer-book.

The story of another of our Zulu lads will not be uninteresting before passing on again to the conclusion of Mrs. Wilkinson's letters from Zululand. Though kind and full of love to all the natives, she was especially fond of, successful in the treatment of, the boys and young men of the station. To tell somewhat of them and their doings amongst us is to tell of those who were largely influenced for good by her.

There are many in England who, while taking an interest in Mission work amongst the heathen, seem to have but little idea of the *nature* of that work. They know nothing of what a Mission station really is, how the missionaries pass their days, the troubles and trials we experience with our native converts, as well as the joy and gladness they bring to us; the backsliding; the growings in grace of these sons and daughters in Christ. They know nothing of the way in which we gain one by one to the Church of God, here a little and there a little, those through whom, year by year, our stations, small at first, increase and make their presence felt in the midst of a heathen land. To such I would say that our Mission stations—as they necessarily at first must be—are few and far between. Forty or fifty miles is no uncommon distance between one missionary and his brother who labours next to him in the Mission field.

From Kwamagwaza, for instance, our Zulu headquarters, we had to ride a distance of 200 miles to our next station northwards on the edge of the Amaswazi country. The object which I constantly kept before me was the forging of a chain of Mission stations, from the

Tugela River towards the River Zambesi, planting those stations at a distance of some forty miles apart one from the other, which is a fair day's ride in that part of the world. Round these stations I hoped to place, as time went on, native stations overlooked by native ministers, into which I trusted to see the lads, I daily trained, grow by God's grace. Such a distance places the missionary, upon any one station, in a position to hold communication with one or more of his brother missionaries by a day's journey on horseback. This is no small consideration in a country so wide and wild as South Africa, where human help in times of distress and trouble is so sorely needed; though often vain, in such cases, is the help of man.

But it may be asked. Why allow so long a link to exist in what should be a closely wrought chain of equi-distant stations? The answer must be that in South Africa, as in other parts of the world, we are not always, or by any means, our own masters. We cannot always be and do what we would. My application to Cetewayo for sites upon which to found Mission stations in his kingdom, by which the most southerly Amaswazi station might be linked up with Kwamagwaza, was refused upon the score that the king considered the number of stations in his country were quite sufficient, and he did not wish to see them increased. There were chiefs in this intermediate tract of country who would have welcomed us amongst their people; but as Cetewayo was ever the final court of appeal in such and all important cases, the accomplishment of the object which I so much desired was denied me.

To neglect on this account the Amaswazi and Amatonga kingdoms, which were embraced in the diocese of Zululand as defined not only by the Royal license, which sent a Bishop to Zululand and to the country of the tribes towards the Zambezi River,' but as laid down by the Provincial Synod of South Africa, would have been denying the Gospel to that people because the Zulu king denied it to his own people. All the more strongly, it seemed to me, did our duty lie towards the Amaswazi, upon Scriptural grounds, because further entrance was denied us amongst the Zulus. '*Seeing ye put it from you, and judge yourselves unworthy of everlasting life, lo, we turn to the Gentiles.*' But I must not forget the promised story of my Zulu boy.

There came to work upon the Kwamagwaza station a lad who was afterwards baptized by the name of Peter. His *kraal* was situated some seventeen miles distant, in the valley of the Umthlatuzi River. He was a fine lad, but with an expression of countenance which indicated a wilful temper, and one difficult to deal with. In due course, and after due training he was baptized. The work appointed him upon the station, under Mr. Adams, our lay superintendent, was of that general kind which forms the employment of natives upon the Mission stations of South Africa.

A Mission station is by no means unlike an English farmstead, and grateful is the sight, after a long day's ride through the heathen wild, to come suddenly over some hillside upon one of these peaceful Christian villages nestling amongst their fruit and gum trees, with the missionary's church and house standing up conspicuously in the midst of the Christians' cottages, which are dotted around and within the neighbouring hills and valleys; a light shining verily in a dark place. Upon a well-worked station a technical education will always be found going on side by side with the spiritual education.

Our mission to the heathen is not only to make them Christians, but to make them *useful* and *industrious* Christians, to make them *good* citizens, and a credit to our work in the eyes of the colonists, who value a Christian native not by the amount of book learning he possesses, but for the amount of skilled labour, honestly performed, which he can do beyond his heathen brother. And reasonably so. If we were colonists working hard for our living we should expect the same.

Upon a Mission station, therefore, as upon an English farm, you will see the operations of ploughing, sowing, crop clearing, reaping, fencing, draining, &c. &c., going forward each in its season. And you will find a still larger variety of work on hand, amongst our South African Mission stations, than upon an English farm; for our stations, it must be remembered, are far removed from civilisation, and we cannot call to our assistance carpenters, bricklayers, masons, thatchers, blacksmiths, and such-like craftsmen. When we require this class of labour we must *find it amongst ourselves*, and to find it we must first *create* it.

Our principal aim, therefore, after due attention to the spiritual work, is to instruct our natives in all these crafts, and there is never lack of opportunity for trying their hands at all of them. There is no lack of work for skilled hands to do, if a station has been established some years, and is doing a good work. A station is, or ought to be, ever on the increase. New buildings of one kind or another are added year by year, and existing buildings are always needing some repair, more frequently than we can find hands to execute them. The Zulus are not only apt, but very anxious to learn the arts and crafts of the while man's civilisation, and many become most proficient in them. One of the best blacksmiths in Durban is a Zulu. I saw one of the two houses being built at Rorke's Drift, which were so gallantly defended by a handful of our soldiers, and it was being built by Zulus; Mr. Rorke raising the corners only, and leaving the rest to native hands.

A house was built for me at Pretoria by an Usutu, who became a Christian upon the German station in that town, who four years before had come into Pretoria a heathen clothed in skins! The parsonage of a native station, near Kwamagwaza, which is frequently mentioned in these letters, was entirely built by our native Christians, overlooked by a half caste, whom I placed at the head of the work. They got out the brick earth, made the bricks, burnt them, and built the house. Again, one of our Christians, who when I first arrived at Kwamagwaza, had never handled a plane or a chisel, was able in a year's time, under the instruction of our young carpenter, Mr. Hales, to do all the odd rough carpentering jobs upon the station. Where is the English labourer who could do all this?

Such was the varied work of one kind or other that Peter was set to do when he came to the station. He was, however, a bad worker—idle, wilful, and unsatisfactory. He would shirk his work on every possible occasion. He would run away and hide in the long grass for days together, rather than set himself to do an honest day's work; and, like the unfortunate man of Gadara, who had his dwelling amongst the tombs, '*no man could tame him.*' Such was the material we had frequently to deal with in the young Zulus who came to us. At last, in Peter's case, things came to such a pass that it was thought well, not only on his own account, but for example's sake, to punish him severely. This was done, and I then spoke to him seriously of his evil doings, and begged him to turn over a new leaf, and try to set a better example to the other lads upon the station. I urged him to do his work honestly, and be a comfort and help to us, instead of a sorrow and a hindrance. This was in the year 1873.

I was just then forming a class of candidates for Confirmation, and urged him to join it. He did so, and was amongst the most regular and promising in the class. He was a very clever young fellow, and his questions and answers would have put to shame many a candidate for Confirmation here in England. After Confirmation he became a communicant, and was doing so well, both in school and out of it, that I placed him in a class of young men, whom I was training with a view to a native ministry. Every afternoon he wrote, amongst his other studies, an essay or exposition upon some part of either Old or New Testament history. I wish I had kept these, that I might now give a specimen of them—some were very good.

Upon one occasion, when writing upon our Blessed Lord's sufferings, I found him with his head upon his hands, and the tears running down his cheeks. It was impossible not to become attached to this young fellow, so troublesome and unmanageable as he had once been, and now so greatly improved. He was a member of our native choir, and although he had not much idea of singing, he learnt his notes with remarkable quickness.

It happened about this time that a heathen lad on the station charged him with a very grave offence, an offence of which we discovered by investigation he was entirely innocent. He took the matter, however, so much to heart that, without signifying his intention to anyone on the station, he left us and returned to his *kraal*. We heard he was living there, to all outward appearance, like a heathen again. He had cast off his European clothing, which is always adopted with Christianity, and was wearing again his '*mutya*,' or native heathen dress, consisting of a slight girdle of wild beast skins. I sent two of our best Christians to endeavour to persuade him to return, but to no purpose. I began to fear that he would never come back, and my disappointment and vexation were in proportion to the hopes I had entertained of his future.

One Sunday morning, however, several months after his departure, he came into the vestry with the rest of the choir, and put on his surplice. During the service he hung his head very low, and seemed to feel much ashamed of himself. After service I called him aside, and spoke to him very seriously of the step he had taken, and of his subsequent conduct. He was always a lad of few words, but from what I could get out of him, I gathered that he had felt so acutely the charge laid against, him, and feared so much that we should believe it, and thus lose our confidence in him, that he had gone away as I have related. It was both foolish and wrong, but these young Christians find it hard to fight against those difficulties and temptations which we so often find act as stumbling blocks and occasions of falling to our English lads at home, Christians though they be through many generations of Christianity.

The story of Joseph's temptation and imprisonment for righteousness' sake, occurring in the lessons for the day, I spoke to him upon that subject, and drew from it a lesson suiting his own case. I am quite sure that amidst that heathen life, to which he had for a time returned, he was utterly dissatisfied with himself and everything around him.

Day by day he would see and hear sights and sounds that would be gall and bitterness to one who had tasted of those high and blessed mysteries to which he was no stranger, and I can look upon his return to us in no other light than the result of the witness of the Holy Spirit within him, drawing him away from heathen scenes, back to that pure, good Christian life which he had left, and which could alone bring again rest unto his soul.

It was no fortuitous circumstance which had brought him back to us, late that Saturday evening. He had, I believe, been counting the Sundays as they passed, and could not bear to be away another, and thus had planned his return, in order to be with us on the Sunday, as I have related. Since that time he has, I believe, been going on satisfactorily, and will, I trust, one day, by God's blessing, if my plan in life for him is kept in view, be a fellow-Helper in the Church of God in Zululand.

We now return to Mrs. Wilkinson's remaining letters from Zululand.

St Mary's, Zululand, Dec. 14, 1873.

On Saturday we hope to have the Church consecrated, and on Sunday Mr. Carlson, Martyn, and William (the two natives) will, I hope, be ordained deacons. You may see by the papers that there has been fighting in Natal between the Government and the *kafirs*. It is only one rebellious chief—Langalibalele; another chief aided him to escape, but our people very soon *settled him*, and fined him 2000 head of cattle. Three volunteers were killed at the first. The major in command had orders not to fire the first shot, but they were hemmed in. It was a very sad affair; since that, however, our troops have had little difficulty. Though they have not yet caught Langalibalele himself, they have taken 1,500 of his women and 9,000 of his cattle, besides numbers of sheep, goats, and horses. The women they have bound out to the colonists for three years; this is a great gain to them, for there is a dreadful scarcity of labour in the colony. Crops of sugar, coffee, and cotton lying in the fields, because there are no hands to harvest them. The diamond fields have attracted hundreds of the natives.

The gold fields are progressing; we hear they have found a nugget weighing twenty, one pounds. Pretoria lies between the diamond and the goldfields, and now a road is being made to Delagoa Bay. At present all goods have to be brought by ox waggon from Durban; if you look at the map you will see the immense advantage this will be to Pretoria. This is since we were there, so that property increases in value most rapidly.

The map will show that Delagoa Bay is the natural mouth for imports and exports to and from the Transvaal. The railway scheme taken up so warmly by President Burgers from the Bay to Pretoria, but which he failed to accomplish, was being taken in hand again by English enterprise before the disastrous restoration of the Transvaal to the Boers. Now all such progress is at an end of course.

St. Mary's, Zululand, Fest. Holy Innocents, 1873.
I have had the house full of visitors. That *at home* involves some trouble, but here, where one is cook and hostess in one, it is rather overwhelming. The week before Christmas all the Samuelsons arrived. Five adults and three little ones. On the Friday, Mr. Jackson and Mr. Carlson from Amaswaziland. On Saturday, December 20, our dear little church and yard were consecrated. We had such an extremely nice service, and a beautiful day. Our choir in surplices for the first time. They came in procession from the school, and were met at the door by Mr. Robertson who presented the petition for consecration to the Bishop, and then they came up the church singing the 24th Psalm. They chanted all the Psalms capitally, 84th, 122nd, 132nd. Mr. Samuelson preached.
On Sunday, 21st (St. Thomas), the Bishop ordained Mr. Carlson, Martyn, and William Heber, deacons. They sat in chairs before the Bishop, and after laying on of hands Mr. J. took them into the vestry and robed them. William Heber read the Gospel. It was a very happy day. E. has translated Hymns Ancient and Modern, so we were able to sing appropriate hymns in Zulu on this and every occasion. On Monday I unceremoniously left half of my guests to take care of themselves and rode with E., Mr. Jackson, and Mr. Carlson, to see the new parsonage-house at Empandhleni (SS. Philip and James station).
It has been built entirely by John Fea, the half-caste, and our native boys, and it reflects the greatest credit on them. The house is of a burnt brick, the other wattle and daub. We came home next morning, and amused ourselves by racing till our horses got so excited we could hardly hold them in when going qui-

etly. Thursday, Christmas Day, was rather showery, but we had a nice service. The choristers, five clergy, and the Bishop made rather an imposing sight in our usually dull services, but now we have a nice church it will be different.

Yesterday E. started back with Mr. Jackson and Martyn to Amaswaziland. He has gone to see about the land for Martyn's station, where we also shall live for part of the year. Today they are resting with a very nice old Norwegian missionary and his wife, whom we stayed with on our first journey up. Tomorrow they will reach Intaba 'Nkulu. Tuesday, at the German Mission and settlement of Luneberg on the Pongolo River, and Wednesday at the Amaswazi station. So they will have no *kraal* life, which is a great comfort.

This letter ends the year 1873; a year which altered very much the lines of the Mission work in the diocese of Zululand. Cetewayo, after his coronation, becoming more and more overbearing and intolerant, set himself more determinately against missionaries and their work than ever. He refused all applications for new sites for stations, and having turned the German missionaries out of the country, said openly that he wished all the missionaries to go. That he would have turned us out had he dared to do so, there can be no doubt. Henceforward it was evident that if any progress was to be made in Mission work in that diocese, it could only be by carrying the work northwards out of his kingdom. This was admissible so long as the work was not carried beyond the 26th parallel of S. latitude, which, as has been already stated, is the northern boundary of the diocese as laid down by the Provincial Synod.

CHAPTER 12

Northward of Zululand

St. Mary's, Zululand, Jan. 6, 1874.

Yesterday, William Heber, one of the newly ordained native deacons, took the morning prayers, and preached in the evening. He looks so nice in his surplice and blue stole. He is as tall as Mr. Robertson, and all the Zulus have a fine bearing.

It is a lovely starlight evening. I have just come in, contrasting our state with that of the colonists, for no woman dare go out alone after sunset in the colony, the *Kafirs* are so corrupted by the white man. It must be so, for no Zulu here would dream of touching a woman, far less a white one. Mrs. Robertson is very poorly, and cannot move off the sofa. Mr. R. is very anxious about her. One cannot get a doctor up here. When I was so ill two years ago, E. tried, but money would not bring them. I believe he offered *50l.*, or any sum they chose to ask.

Do you remember my telling you of all the killing that went on near us, and of a great friend of ours being obliged to fly, and also that we heard he had been killed? I saw him today. He has been hiding away, and now is forgiven by the king. He was on his way to the great annual war dance. Many go by each day. It is astonishing to see the number of guns that go by: there must be thousands now in the country. We must keep powder flasks out of their hands if possible. They use a cow horn, but when they get excited they waste a great deal of powder in this way.

The number of guns was no doubt increasing very rapidly at this time in Zululand, and although we have to thank traders in the contraband of guns, powder, and caps from Natal for arming the Zulus (as it has eventually turned out against ourselves), we have to thank Delagoa Bay for much more of this evil. Until we hold that most *important*, and to us *essential*, seaport we shall never be in a position to keep the tribes of this part of the interior from arming themselves against the white man. The Portuguese may promise, but they cannot fulfil their promises. They are too weak even if they had the will to do so.

St. Mary's, Zululand, Jan. 8, 1874.

Little Edie is not spoilt by the Zulu children. the other day her greatest friend told her with great contempt that she was "only a little white child." She was eating roughly the other day, and Elizabeth her old black nurse told her she was like a little pig. "*Qa! Mame,*" she replied, "*angiyingolubi, ngiyikolwa.*" (No, mother, I am not a pig, I am a Christian.)

E. has gone off again to Amaswaziland. Two years ago it was an unknown country, and we often laugh when we think what a circuit Mr. Robertson made with E. to avoid the "fever country." I believe they were nearly three weeks getting up, and now E. and I ride it in four days. It could be done in three, but we go a little out of the way in order to sleep at a mission station instead of a *kraal*. There is no fever country near, it is all high land. E. has gone to look at some land which he means to buy in order to make a new station. It is in the Transvaal, but on the borders of Amaswaziland. The Amaswazi princes will not let a missionary go into their country to live; but we are far better off out of it on our own land, where we can do as we like and are not fettered as we are here. Mr. Jackson at the Amaswazi station has already several lads who wish to become Christians. Here in Zululand the king does not like them to come to work even at a mission station, and every convert is gained with great struggles.

E. left two days after Christmas day; I hope he may be back in ten days more. He may be stopped by the rivers which rise very quickly at this time of the year. The Carlsons were kept waiting at the side of a river three weeks. Can you imagine anything so wearying? The river would be fast going down one day, and they would go to bed intending to cross next day. Then there would come a thunderstorm up in the hills and the river would be as high as ever. We shall have nothing of this in going up to the Transvaal, for the rains will be over; indeed that is all we are waiting for. They have found a nugget at the goldfields weigh-

155

ing 21 lbs. I expect E. has gone off there; I know be was anxious to see the fields, and I also know that a gentleman was going to drive them there after he had seen E.

The river here alluded to by which the Carlsons were stopped for three weeks was the Intombi, the river beside which poor Captain Moriarty and his force, in coming from Mr. Jackson's Amaswazi station at Derby with a convoy of waggons, was outspanned when attacked and destroyed by Umbelini. It is a small, but deep and very troublesome river. No one, without experience, can have any idea of the discomfort of being outspanned for any length of time beside a river in the rainy season, waiting for the waters to abate. The whole neighbourhood of the waggon gets trampled into mud by the feet of the oxen which must be collected and tied up to the waggon at night.

A fire cannot be lighted to cook by. The waggon tilt, the bedding inside, and everything in fact gets damp and smells most disagreeably. Such a state of damp, discomfort, and inaction, coupled often with want of proper food, not unfrequently results in fever, which adds terribly to the misery of the situation. Here is the disadvantage of travelling by ox waggon in the rainy season. If on horseback it is a small matter comparatively to put your horse at the river and make a venture of it. I was once rolled over with my horse when attempting to swim the Bivane River near where Sir Evelyn Wood's camp at Kambula afterward stood. I had a cassock on, tied up round my waist, which hindered my swimming; and to add to the difficulty I got my foot entangled in the stirrup. In consequence of this delay I missed the drift on the opposite side by being carried down the river, through the violence of the stream, to a point where the banks stood up like walls, and I was very nearly being drowned.

St. Mary's, Zululand, Jan. 31, 1874.

This morning I had a horrid fright for a few minutes. I was told that Martyn had returned, *and alone*. You can imagine how my heart went. I had been getting a little fidgety, for E. has been away five weeks today. I send you his letter, as it will describe his doings far better than I can. I had intended tearing off the last part, but think you may be amused at the description of *our* way of travelling as compared with yours. The two front oxen are always led by a long string, and the rest follow in their footsteps. Is not E.'s description of the weather up north lovely? Here there have been plenty of wet days. A thunderstorm last week was very severe. At a *kraal* about fifteen miles off, forty cattle were struck down dead at once. The Natal affairs are comfortably settled. They have caught the old rebel, but the volunteers had some very rough work amongst the mountains, going up and down, six, seven, ten, eleven thousand feet high, bitterly cold although the height of summer.

Martyn says he never saw E. so happy as he was at the *kraal* which is on the land bought for the second Amaswazi station. The Amaswazi were always bringing nice pots of fresh milk &c., and they gave Martyn much more than he could eat and drink. Rather a difference to the Zulus. I have my hands full in prospect of the start for the Transvaal. I don't know where to begin. Oh! the picking out things for the waggon journey! Fancy all the children's clothes that will be wanted. And oh! the *dirt* of waggon travelling.

The letter referred to, which describes the country &c. about the second Amaswazi station, which lay considerably to the north of the first, ran as follows:—

Amaswazi station, Derby, Jan. 24, 1874.

You will be glad, I know, to see Martyn and to hear from him what we have been doing since we left you. I send him home as he has matters to settle he tells me, and I can dispense with his help while at the Bombo. We had a good deal of riding about amongst the Dutch before I could fix upon a place suitable for the new station; but at last I bought 6,000 acres for 426*l*. (price first asked 800*l*.), with which I am much pleased. It lies behind Hamilton on the waggon track down to the Udidini flat and the Bombo. About three and a half hours on horseback from Mr. Bell's lands you are on the place. If the railway should run on the ridge—originally intended—between Delagoa Bay and Pretoria we shall be well placed for taking a ticket, doing our shopping, and getting back to tea!

The land is situated partly on the Berg or high flat *veldt*, and is good for sheep. The middle portion lies where the Berg begins to break, which is good for horses, cattle, sheep, mealies, and corn, with firewood in abundance. The third portion lies down lower still, where—being nearly on a level with the Umkomati itself—it is very hot, and capable of yielding tropical produce.

The place is exceedingly well situated for our work. It lies about eighty miles due north of this station and is more closely placed upon the edge of the Amaswazi border, indeed there are Amaswazi *kraals* upon the place itself, it being an extreme border farm on the very edge of the last lands Government can sell without taking a part of the Amaswazi kingdom proper. It is situated on what is called the break of the Berg (the Drakensberg), that is to say, where the high level table land of the Berg breaks down into the rough Umkomati valley, which flowing through Amaswaziland and cutting the Bombo north of Josanas *kraal* enters the sea, I believe, just north of Delagoa Bay.

Near the lower portion of the land, and lying out on the Umkomati valley, is situated one of the Royal Inkosikazi's (Princesses) *kraals*; Umakathlela her name. I think she is one of the old king Umswazi's sisters, but I not quite sure. I stayed for three nights at one of the *kraals* on the place, for indeed there was nowhere else to stay, and found the people very friendly. One of the days of our stay was Sunday; Martyn preached to them a very good sermon, and appropriate for such as had never, as they told us, heard such "*Izindaba*" (news) before. I intend to have a couple or three little houses put up for Martyn, and another family or two whom we shall perhaps find willing to come with us from Kwamagwaza, but shall delay a little building our own house, perhaps a few months, as we cannot do everything at once.

The site I have chosen for the station is very pretty, and I think as fertile as any part of the district. A great ridge of brown, round ironstone rocks runs along upon one side for about four English miles, with a *spruit* of good water at the foot of it. On the other side of the *spruit* is a gentle slope, where the station will stand, extending the entire length of the ridge of rock. At the further end the *spruit* referred to meets another, which comes bouncing down between some steep rocks in a series of little cascades. Exactly at the point of junction the two *spruits* fling their combined waters down an exceedingly pretty little gorge, forming a fine fall, very steep and rocky, and slightly wooded. The peep between shows the Umkomati valley, and beyond a *wild wild* toss of country deep into Amaswaziland, blue, rugged mountains, and full of feature.

When the combined streams reach the bottom, at about two

hundred and fifty feet, they flow on together, are joined by a few smaller *spruits* in the next valley, and there is a series of cascades of at least 350 to 400 feet; they whirl away together into a wooded *kloof*, which in a very short time passes them on to the Umkomati itself.

I propose to build our house just above the point of junction of the two *spruits*, so that the garden will run down to the waterfall, and be supplied and watered by the *spruit* behind. I look forward to the day when we shall sit together with the bairns at tea under the fruit trees, listening to the sound of the falling water coming and going on the evening air. We shall be two days' horseback journey from Lydenburg, three good days from Pretoria, one and a half from Udidini (the Royal Amaswazi *kraal*), and about two or two and a half from the Bombo. A fine central position for a large amount of Mission work which please God may be in the future.

I met your friends Hampson and Compton returning from Lydenburg to Durban. They have finished their section of the Delagoa Bay road, and pronounce it open for traffic from Lydenburg to the Bombo. Other contractors are taking it through the Bombo above Josanas twenty-four miles at 30*l*. per mile, after which it runs on the flat to Delagoa Bay. They report 500 diggers at the fields; provisions fabulous, the great nugget a hoax (three pounds instead of thirteen), but progress fair. Mr. Jackson left us the last ten days of our stay on the Umkomati. He came down to turn some builders back to me whom we had met trekking here from Pretoria seeking work.

We tried a short cut to the Glen from the Umkomati, instead of returning to Hamilton and taking the waggon track, got into a terribly rough country somewhere amongst the Swazi, old Martyn becoming more bewildered the further we went astray, and ended by sleeping out on the *veldt* on a steep and very stony, and therefore not very comfortable, hillside. We lost our bag of tea, finished our coffee, and were unable, in the dark, to get any water. However, I had a pot of Liebig about one-third full, into which Martyn and myself alternately dipped our fingers, pronounced excellent, and laid down to sleep.

I am delighted with this exquisite summer climate on the high *veldt*; it is like the most beautiful cool English summer weather, no wind, and though absent a month today never stopped one hour by the rain. The air is clear, thin, cool, and delicious beyond description. I despise Kwamagwaza, and all its nasty winds, and mists, and rain. Would that you could enjoy this with me! Such lovely mornings and evenings, and a midday tempered to perfection with just a breeze. I have experienced some European climates, but none so perfect as this.

I want to pack up the waggons and start, immediately upon my return. I see a great deal of work before me up here in Amaswaziland and in the Transvaal, which 1874 will be all too short to get through well, and I have nothing more to do in Zululand, therefore I want you to be acting for me in these matters, that there will be no delay when I come.'

Mrs. Carlson is now in charge of this beautiful station upon the Umkomati River, which we had hoped to make our headquarters upon our return to Africa. The Amaswazi stations are still at work, whilst our missionaries in Zululand have, during the war, been all obliged to leave their work. The beautiful climate to the north of Zululand, which it is hoped extends, as the high land extends, to the Zambesi itself, is full of promise for the future work we have in hand when the Delagoa Bay Bishopric shall be founded.

St. Mary's, Zululand, Feb. 25, 1874.
Ophthalmia has been very prevalent here, and both children have had slight attacks. I have been very bad with one of my eyes. I suffered dreadfully for a night and a day till I tried alum. It had a marvellous effect, and the great pain was gone in half an hour. Six grains in one ounce of water. My eye was discharging, and a splitting headache. I was four days in bed in quite a dark room, and was so miserable and lonely with only Zulus about me. We hope to move north in about three weeks, but our oxen are dying of lung sickness. I am looking forward to the change for Putu, hoping that it may do her good.

So poor Dr. Livingstone is really dead; all alone out there, without having reaped the glories due to him and which would have been showered upon him at home.

I hope you have suffered no uneasiness on our account about the rebellion in Natal. We have heard nothing of it here except through the papers, and now it is quite at an end. The volunteers had some very rough and trying work following the rebel chief through the mountains. They have spared his life, but are going to banish him to Robben Island which is close to Cape-town. It is said that Cetewayo refused to help him. He is afraid of the English Government, or rather, afraid of losing their support and countenance, for he is not a friend of the Boers who bound his kingdom on the north.

We have two pineapples ripe in the garden. We are proud, as Mr. Robertson never succeeded with them. We have also one coffee berry, and twelve young oranges. But our trees are quite young. However, this shows that with care they may be grown up on these hills. The great labour here is to keep down the weeds in summer. In two months' time they are up to your waist. We have just now in the garden the most perfectly pure white hibiscus. We have it as a low fence on one of the terraces. We were obliged to have some little protection, otherwise the children would be rolling down. This flower looks so well in the vases in church mixed with a red plant, a kind of amaran-thus, which grows here and is very handsome. We always talk to little Edie in English, and she understands, but always replies in Zulu unless prompted, and then it is Zulu-English.

It is stated in this letter that Cetewayo refused to help Langalibalele, the rebel chief of Natal. It was found out afterwards however that he had invited him into Zululand. Langalibalele was reputed to be a great rainmaker, and it was under pretence of wanting rain in Zululand, but really, doubtless, to favour the rebel, that Cetewayo asked him to come up to him. There can be no doubt that wherever in South Africa rebellion and insubordination have existed since Cetewayo came into power, if he has not been at the bottom of it, he has been at its side, encouraging it by his messages of approval and goodwill.

Pretoria, Transvaal, April 20, 1874.
You will like to hear a little about our journey. It was an unu-sually wet season, but we were most highly favoured. I do not think we were stopped twelve hours through the whole jour-ney by rain. To have wet weather in a waggon is simply abomi-nable; one cannot move, for it makes the necks of the oxen sore with the yoke. So you have to sit in the waggon and watch the rain and long for it to cease, and when you pitch the tent the long grass is all wet.

One night we had a tremendous thunderstorm. I was sleeping in the tent with the children, and in a few minutes we were lying in pools of water. As soon as it abated we all scrambled into the waggon and sat there until it was light enough to trek on. The first river we came to upon the Transvaal border was a very bad one to cross, very steep sides, and a rocky bottom. Just as we got to it a tremendous thunderstorm came on with torrents of rain. We found a German waggon sticking in the river with another to follow; night was coming on, the river was rapidly rising, and these wretched Germans were making the opposite bank as slippery as ice in their struggles to get up.

However, by the time they were out the rain was over, and in we went with twenty-eight oxen, so that the front ones might have a firm footing, whilst the others struggled in the water. I dare not ride down this steep bank, and when I did get in, the waggon looked as if it must go over so tilted up was it on one side. But we crossed safely, after such a bumping and jolting over the boulders, and outspanned on the other side.

The next river, the Pongolo, a large one, and the boundary between the Transvaal and Zululand, was very high. We went in with twenty-eight again, but the river was so high and the current so strong the oxen had to swim, and the front ones could not get away fast enough from the hinder ones, so there they were all huddled together with legs over trek-tow chain and yokes twisted. So we sat in the river whilst the men were getting the oxen's legs back again, no easy matter when the river was breast high with a strong current. Such a shouting and uproar, the black bodies of the natives mixed with the struggling oxen, the cracking of whips, and roar of the waters. We had about eight inches of water in the waggon , but we all crossed safely and outspanned, for it was dark. We left Martyn and his family with our tent on the new station on the Umkomati River to begin the work.

You must not think all the Transvaal is in Bishop Webb's diocese, a very large slice is in E.'s; all East of the Drakensberg range, which runs north and south, in spite of what maps may say to the contrary. Pretoria is about 120 miles from the nearest point of his diocese. People at home would be rather astonished to hear this. We only arrived here four days ago, and are still in the confusion of settling, and I have no one to help me, except that E. is a host in himself. Ladies always remark how different he is in that respect to most gentlemen, who get out of the work and leave it all to their wives. But Putu cannot bear me out of her sight, and a most miserable wail is immediately set up if she comes into the room and finds me flown, "*Ngiyafuna Inkosikazi*" (I want the chieftainess); and if anyone else comes near to supply my place sweeps them all away, working her out-stretched arms and exclaiming, "*Angitandi, angitandi*" (I don't like you, I don't like you), and this even to *her father*.

This is a most horribly expensive place. Kid gloves 6s. a pair, soap 1s. 6d. per lb. No wonder the Dutch are such dirty people. We have three cows with us; their calves were all born upon the road. For instance, we stop in the middle of the day for two hours for dinner; the boy comes and says, "One of the cows is going to calve!" At the end of the two hours we go on again, and we see a little calf running with its mother, and it goes on with us for about another twelve miles!

The Amaswazi country, upon the edge of which we travelled upon this journey to Pretoria, was at this time in a very disturbed state. It is an almost trackless district, and we managed to lose ourselves for three days in the flat open veldt beyond the Pongolo River. The king being a minor, the country was ruled by his uncles. One of these, Umd-wandwe, was a very bad fellow, who endeavoured to bribe one of the young king's servants to poison him. This man's intrigues, which were discovered at this time, brought about his own death together with many of his tribe. The queen mother, an exceedingly fine-looking and intelligent woman, discovered the plot. She summoned all the young king's uncles, together with the great chiefs of the country, to Udidini, the royal *kraal*.

Here, at a signal given by her, Umdwandwe fell, as he was at-tempting to fly to the stream below the *kraal*, covered with *assegais*. The queen mother then despatched an *impi* of her warriors to destroy this man's tribe. Four thousand fell in one night, and, as an example of the cool forethought of these people, *impis* were ordered to post themselves at various points of exit from the Amaswazi country to despatch fugitives to Natal and the Transvaal; just, in fact, as sportsmen place guns at the comers of coverts where the game is likely to run out and get away.

We arrived at Mr. Jackson's station just after this great slaughter. The station is situated upon the edge of the country occupied by Umdwandwe's tribe. We found the members of the Amaswazi mission, together with a few English settlers from the neighbourhood, in a state of much anxiety. For several nights they had set up a guard expecting the station would be attacked, with guns piled, and ammunition ready for use at a moment's notice. The *émeute*, however, passed away in time, and tranquillity was restored without further bloodshed. Many of the bodies were lying in the bushes not far from the station, and became food for vultures and jackals.

CHAPTER 13

Journeyings in the Transvaal

Pretoria, Transvaal, July 10, 1874.

E. left me yesterday for another month's visitation. We have altered our plans a little. E. says he must go down to Zululand and see poor Mr. Robertson, who has lost his wife, before leaving for England, so we may be delayed a couple of months. I wonder whether you will think we have grown *Colonial*, I know that we have grown more *practical*. I shall be dreadfully disappointed if I do not go home by the diamond fields. I have been promised fifty loads of earth to sort, and that out of one of the richest claims on the fields. E. meant to have brought home a small barrel of *unsorted* earth, and then at Christmas time bring it out and divide it into as many parcels as persons present.

What a capital game of "grab" it would have made. I think Dr. C. has *done for himself* in the Colony; he will never be able to remain. I suppose you have seen in the papers that he says Langalibalele had not a fair trial, and is trying to upset the decision of the court. It will be a terrible thing for Natal if he succeeds, for the natives have no idea of an appeal—a decision is a decision. He has a lot of sentimental nonsense on the subject of the native. If the Government had not acted promptly and decidedly there is no knowing how far the rebellion might have spread.

You cannot punish a *Kafir* more severely than by "eating him up"—*i.e.* taking his cattle from him. They much prefer death. They now think that Langalibalele was dealt with very leniently—or rather they would say amongst themselves that the Government were *afraid* to put him to death. By all their ideas of right and wrong he should have been killed, so they will think

165

it a still greater sign of weakness if he should be set free.'

The reversing of the Colonial sentence upon Langalibalele by the Home Government had a very bad effect indeed upon the native mind in South Africa. Perhaps it may not be too much to say that the late Zulu War is to a certain extent the outcome of that mistaken policy. Cetewayo boasted that the English would never fight him, that they were always talking and never acting, and that they settled everything by arbitration and conferences.

The two visitations referred to in this letter lay, the one through the western and southern Transvaal, by Rustenburg, Zerrust, Lichtenberg, and Potchefstrom, a circuit of some 400 to 500 miles. Zeerust is no very great distance from Dr. Livingstone's old mission station of Kolobeng, upon the edge of the Kalihari desert. The other lay through the north and eastern Transvaal by the Erstelling goldfields, and thence through Secocoeni's country to Lydenburg, the goldfields of Pilgrim's Rest and of Mac Mac, and thence back through Middelburg to Pretoria, about 700 miles. Secocoeni was just breaking into that rebellion against the Government of the Transvaal Republic which ended in the loss of the Presidentship by Mr. Burgers, and the annexation of the Transvaal by the British Government.

I was strongly warned by the Dutch not to pass from Erstelling to Lydenburg through Secocoeni's country, but the circuit which it would have been necessary to make in order to avoid it would have been far too great. As it turned out we were not molested either by him or his people, and had the advantage of seeing some of his vast mountain strongholds, from which first the Dutch, and then we ourselves had so much difficulty in dislodging him. He was already calling his people, women, children, and cattle, up into these fastnesses, preparatory to his intended resistance to the Boers. The magistrate at Lydenburg, Mr. Cooper, asked me upon my arrival at that place to go back with him and visit Secocoeni, and endeavour to open friendly relations with him. This I was unable to do, as I had much work on my hands, and little time to do it in.

It has been repeatedly asserted that the Zulu War was the result of the Transvaal annexation. I believe no statement could be more untrue. I venture to think that few had better opportunities of knowing the tone and intentions of the native mind than ourselves. We were at that time in constant intercourse not only with natives in and on the borders of the Transvaal, but also with the Zulus, staying as we did for days and weeks in their *kraals*. Of this, at all events, I am quite certain, that Cetewayo and Secocoeni were resolved to act in concert; the former was massing his forces with a view to enter upon, the south-eastern border of the Transvaal, and Secocoeni was preparing to come down from his strongholds in the north Transvaal, the concerted plan being to sweep *every Dutchman out of the Republic.*

What could we have done in such an issue, with so much British life and property at stake in the Transvaal? Could we have looked on at all this and done nothing? and yet what force had we then in South Africa to prevent it? We should have been drawn into a far more terrible war than that in which we were lately engaged in Zululand, inasmuch as Secocoeni would have been against us as well as the Zulus, and we should have had but a handful of troops to withstand their joint attack. That we might have been crushed out of Natal is possible. That the wave of war and rebellion might have swept *beyond* Natal onward toward the Cape Colony, or even Capetown itself, is also possible, and that our South African colonies might have seen reproduced in their midst the horrors of the Indian Mutiny of 1857 is what *might have been.*

As it was, we stepped in and stemmed the terrible tide by the annexation of a Republic which could neither rule itself nor the natives around it. That the annexation of the Transvaal *delayed* rather than *precipitated* the Zulu War is much nearer the truth than the reverse. That Cetewayo's attitude towards us after the annexation was entirely changed is quite true. But the reason is not far to seek. We thereby hemmed him in; it was no longer possible for him to break forth either against Boer or native except through British territory. If he was now to 'wash his spears'—which can alone seal the accession to the Zulu throne and make him a true king in the eyes of his people—it could only be done in *English* blood, and in English blood he was at last determined they should be washed.

Hence our late trouble; a trouble from which we can never be permanently safe until we have not only taken the Zulu country under our own government, but obtained from the Portuguese Delagoa Bay, which has been the port through which the thousands and hundreds of thousands of guns and ammunition-cases have passed into Zulu hands. Anything short of this will but find us in a few years in precisely the same situation again as we lately were, or worse, since the Zulus will every year become better armed and disciplined against us. If we send Cetewayo back to Zululand the evil will be precipitated.

E. has ridden today to Heidelberg to give the inhabitants a service. It is about 60 miles, but his one horse that is left (having lost three upon his first visitation) is a splendid little fellow. He carried him one day 91 miles through Secocoeni's country. E. sent him down to me as a present last February, but I have never ventured to mount him; he bucks so. He and his master have many battles; but he has never got E. off yet, though he very nearly succeeded the other day in the market square.

Next Sunday is "*Naacht Maal*" Sunday amongst the Dutch, *i.e.,* Holy Communion, literally "night meal." The market square is fast filling with waggons and tents; there may be about 220 waggons.

E. is building a house on our land opposite this house. It is to be used as a school. Fancy our dismay the other evening when, word was sent us that all the grass which had been cut for the thatch, 1,800 bundles, had been burnt by a grass fire. We are now ready for it; but I hear 4,000 bundles are coming into market tomorrow,

I have not much time for writing now. I have always five to provide for. And then E. constantly brings people down who are passing through, or who have been kind to him on his journeys. We often sit down eight to dinner. Housekeeping here is something frightful. Coarse sugar 1*s.* per lb., flour 5*s.* per lb., bar of soap 2*s.*, and everything else at the same rate.

I saw today a lump of gold that had come down from Marabastadt. It was almost as much as I could hold. I had no idea gold was so heavy, for it was not much larger than a large salt-cellar. It had all been originally gold dust. I think it must have been between 50 and 60 lbs. weight. Gold is so heavy that during the process of washing in a trough you may have a strong stream of water which will wash away large stones, and yet the gold dust will remain at the bottom.

The people here are crying out as the time of our departure draws near. It is time we left, I think, or we should be quite spoilt; everyone is so very kind. This Transvaal climate is magnificent. It is not so wet as Natal and Zululand, and it is much higher also. This winter there was ice on a pond, on which a man stood, and we had ice in a bucket in the kitchen one night. The great drawback to Zululand is the incessant rain. E.

travelled the whole of the wet season this year, and was never kept a day by rain except in Zululand, or rather, I should say, in the neighbourhood of Kwamagwaza. A great many people have settled here who have made money at the diamond fields. It is only four days from here by passenger waggon. I should like to see them and have a sort.

The dearness of every European commodity in the Transvaal is accounted for by the fact that the nearest seaport is Durban, in Natal. All stores have to be brought to Pretoria in ox waggons by a long and tedious land route of some 400 miles. In the rainy season the route is difficult and precarious. In the dry season it is almost impossible to perform the journey, owing to lack of grass for the cattle on the high *veldt*. Delagoa Bay is the natural port for the Transvaal, and until it is in English hands and connected with Pretoria by railway the Transvaal can *never be developed into a prosperous colony*.

This next letter tells of our last trek through Zululand. It may be interesting to know that one of the many *contretemps* which we experienced between Pretoria and Durban on that long and eventful journey, which lasted from October 17 to Christmas Eve, and was borne so patiently and brightly by Mrs. Wilkinson with our poor sick child, was through our waggon sticking fast all one night in the little stony river which flows down from the Udonga, in which the Prince Imperial of France was killed.

I little thought, as we lay in the waggon that night listening to the water as it flowed beneath the waggon, that not far from that spot an event so terrible as the cutting off of that good, pure young life, which filled all Europe with dismay, was one day to be enacted. A wild and desolate district it is; one I have ridden through on horseback and trekked through by ox waggon several times, and was upon each occasion impressed by its weird and dreary aspect.

Knowing so well how greatly these *udongas* or water-washes change their course and appearance with each rainy season, I felt sure that the cairn of stones raised over the place where the prince fell would soon disappear, and the exact spot become difficult to identify. I mentioned this to Sir Evelyn Wood upon his return from Zululand, and he agreed with me, adding, moreover, that the Zulus would be sure to appropriate the stones for building their cattle *kraals* with.

I ventured to represent this to the Empress Eugenie through the Duc de Bassano, and suggested that a strong stone cross should be erected upon the spot, and enclosed by a wall or railing.[1] In answer to my letter I received the following reply from the Duke, which may not be uninteresting—

Camden Place, Chislehurst, 26 *Juillet*, 1879.

Monseigneur,—J'ai mis sous les yeux de Sa Majesté l'Impératrice la lettre que vous m'avez fait l'honneur de m'écrire.

Elle a fait une vive impression sur Sa Majesté, et votre pieuse pensée de marquer par une croix en pierre le lieu du fatal événement qui la plonge dans un si immense douleur, a ému son coeur brisé.

Sa Majesté daigne me donner l'ordre de vous exprimer sa gratitude pour les sentiments qui vous ont inspiré cette pensée si bien d'accord avec sa piété, seule source pour elle de saintes consolations.

L'Impératrice a immédiatement fait écrire au Général Clifford, qui a donné des preuves si touchantes de son attachement à son fils bien aimé, pour le prier de prendre les mesures nécessaires pour l'érection de cette croix, dans le plus court délai possible, à fin qu'elle puisse être placée avant la crue des eaux que vous signalez lors de la saison des pluies. Veuillez, monseigneur, agréer l'hommage de ma haute et respectueuse considération. Bassano.

Amaswazi Station, New Scotland, Fest. All Saints, 1874. Just one line to tell you that we are actually trekking home, I do not know whether we shall have our darling Patu with us. She is very ill. It is her old complaint. If we can but get her to the ship the voyage may restore her. She fell sick three days before we left Pretoria, and we hoped the waggon journey might restore her; but she gets weaker and thinner every day. It is very hard to be reconciled to the thought of losing her. We have had a capital journey so far, and are halfway to Kwamagwaza. We shall stay with Mr. Robertson a month, I think, and then straight for England. Poor Mr. Carlson has lost his wife, and he has a large family. He is living here. One daughter we bring home with us. We hope to leave the Cape about Jan. 10, 1875.

Upon this last journey from Pretoria through Zululand to Durban we had now three infant children to look after: Edith, born at Maritzburg, Annie (or 'Putu,' as the Zulus called her), whom we thought would have died at several points upon the way down; I remember

---

1. This cross was eventually erected by Queen Victoria, and stands upon the spot where the prince fell.

well one evening—when I thought she would not live through the night—walking round the waggon to see if we had a spade with us with which to dig her grave; and Hooper, our 'Boer boy' as we called him, because born at Pretoria among the Boers. This child was but six weeks old when we began that ox waggon journey of some 800 miles, so it may be imagined Mrs. Wilkinson had her hands full. We drove a cow and calf all the way behind the waggon to provide this little fellow with milk; and many a night, and day too, when the calf was too weary to walk, it shared Hoopy's bed in the after part of the waggon, the child and the calf lying nose and nose to one another.

It was upon this journey that the heaviest rain known in East Africa for years fell, and caused such fearfully swollen rivers that when we reached Natal only one bridge was left upon the entire coast line. The Natal coast *abounds* in large and dangerous rivers; and yet every bridge but that one had been swept down into the sea. Zulu huts, dead Zulus, cattle, trees, floating masses of vegetation, and produce of all kinds were carried down daily by the rushing waters. Ours was almost the first waggon that passed down after the flood. The difficulties, therefore, which we experienced in getting across these rivers and cutting out the new drifts, which had been blocked by the floods, it would be impossible to describe.

In one of the largest of these rivers we stuck fast till nightfall, and were only saved from this position by a passing trader, who lent us his span of oxen to assist ours in dragging us out. The danger of being so set fast is that the action of the stream against the wheels forms holes into which they settle, and the waggon heels over. Whilst we were in this predicament the water rose to the floor of the waggon. To keep Mrs. Wilkinson and the children from becoming alarmed I launched bottles upon the river from time to time, and told them to try who could watch them the furthest as they were whirled down.

This is the last letter from Africa. The voyage to England was undertaken with a view to settle some difficulties connected with the extension of the work in the diocese of Zululand, and to report upon the state of Church matters in the Transvaal. This country I had visited at the wish and under the commission of Bishop Webb, who had undertaken the oversight of the Transvaal in addition to his own direct diocesan work in the Orange Free State. It was also hoped to establish a new see to the north of Zululand. When these matters should be settled, a return to Africa was desired as soon as possible.

The result of this visit to England was that the Transvaal bishopric was founded; and the new bishopric of Delagoa Bay, to the north of the diocese of Zululand, has the good wishes of the Metropolitan of South Africa, and awaits the formal sanction of the other bishops of the province in Synod. For this purpose a fund has been opened, and is lodged with the Metropolitan and the provincial trustees of the Church of the Province of South Africa. About 5,000*l.* is already subscribed for its endowment.

In this work Mrs. Wilkinson took the deepest interest. She hoped upon her return to Africa to reside on the high country inland above Delagoa Bay, and was always looking forward to the day when our mission stations from this new centre should reach the Zambesi, the goal of our desires. It was, however, ordered otherwise. Consumption fastened itself upon her towards the end of the year 1877. The disease increased rapidly; it was thought advisable to remove her from S. Devon to Cornwall, with a hope that the climate might restore her again to her work in Africa. But it was not to be. In an exceedingly beautiful spot, than which none more sheltered could perhaps be found upon the coasts of England, she entered into that rest which remaineth to the people of God. She sleeps on the bank of the river Ouse, in the churchyard of Felmersham, in Bedfordshire, the home of her childhood, awaiting that day for which she prayed and laboured, when the kingdoms of this world shall have become the kingdom of our Lord and of His Christ.

One who had shared many a day's journey with us in Africa, the Rev. J. Jackson, the faithful and most successful founder and father of the Amaswazi Mission, wrote as follows upon receiving tidings of her death:—

I cannot begin this note without first saying how sorry I have felt to hear of your very great loss. I have only just now heard the bad tidings here at Derby (Amaswazi station), and when I return home to the Mahamba, and tell our people, I am sure that there is not one of them but will feel and express much sympathy for yourself under the severe trial which you have been called upon to bear. We had begun to hope that better news might come, but this hope is now disappointed. But is not this an earthly wish? Why should we wish to retain amongst us those of His children whom God has long been preparing for His mansions above? The lesson which the event seems to teach us is—Let those who are left do their work as willingly, as vigorously, and as cheerfully as she who is gone did *her* work. *"Where your treasure is, there will your heart be also."*

The Bishop of Maritzburg, with whom she stayed many weeks upon her arrival in Africa, and whom, together with Mrs. Macrorie, she always regarded with much affection, wrote thus:—

How shall I find words to express my sympathy with you, my dear friend, under this heavy blow? I can but assure you that we do feel most deeply for you, and as those only can do who knew something of what you and your dear wife were to one another through all the varied experiences of your life, and that you have our earnest prayers that you may be sustained and comforted in your loneliness of heart with the presence and best consolations of the God of all comfort. Our recollections of your dear wife, whether as we saw her here in 1870 or in those brief peeps in England two years ago, are very sweet and bright. How could they be otherwise?

And we often talk of her with others who knew her in Natal and Zululand; and the thought that rises now as we recall her devoted interest in the work of Christ amongst these poor Zulus, who are now apparently on the eve of strife and bloodshed we cannot tell how terrible, is that her work and prayers cannot be in vain. The labour of the missionaries is, for the present, at a standstill, save amongst the few who are Christians, and who have come out with them across the border, and the last missionary has left Zululand within the past fortnight.

Yet who shall say how many in the rising generation may not have been influenced by the gentle life at Kwamagwaza and the laborious journeys undertaken with such cheerfulness and energy, and in brighter days, which we hope are in store for that now dark land, may live to bless the memory of her who at least prepared the way for the reception of that Gospel which is the stay of their souls for life and death.

CHAPTER 14

Results of Mission Work as Seen Through the Zulu War

The following account of the mission station of Kwamagwaza was written in periodicals and in the daily papers at the time of the Zulu war:—

Under Bishop Wilkinson's hands the station assumed a very busy appearance as the centre of the diocesan work. New buildings, gardens, and avenues of trees sprung up around the settlement, and mission stations were thrown out from it as far north as Amaswaziland and the Transvaal border. In the year 1872 a long range of school buildings was added, and the native college of the diocese, at which promising young Zulus were trained for a native ministry. A beautiful church was also erected in that year, forming one side of the college quadrangle. At its east end was a triple lancet of stained glass.

To this station came many Zulus daily, for it answered the same purpose to Zululand and the Zulus that our monasteries did to the people of these Islands at the dawn of the Christian era. Kwamagwaza was a hospital for the sick and wounded, and a harbour of refuge to those persecuted, afflicted, tormented by the tyrant Cetewayo. Never a day elapsed but some came to that station for assistance of one kind or other, and never went away empty. It was therefore with no surprise, but with great satisfaction, that the following account was read in the *Daily News* from its correspondent at the war time, and dated from Kwamagwaza. His account shows that the Zulus loved the old place, and would have spared it had their imperious king permitted them to do so:—

> The whole of the wounded (in the Battle of Ulundi) went on with the second division. Lord Chelmsford and staff accompanying the flying column. Kwamagwaza was reached on July 11. It was really refreshing to rest our eyes on the one spot in our march through Zululand which bears traces of the hand of civilisation. Plantations of limes, acacias, several sorts of fir, and fruit trees surround the remnants of the church, school, and a few scattered dwelling houses. Paths run through the plantations from these houses to the church. Roses, laburnums, marigolds, and many flowering shrubs border the paths, and larger timber flourishes both in the plantations on the spurs and in grassy *kloofs* of the surrounding hills. Twenty years ago the place was as bare as the surrounding country, so the present beauty bears ample testimony to the capabilities of Zululand, as well as to the loving care of Bishop Wilkinson and the Rev. Mr. Robertson, the founders of the station mission. The people wished to spare the buildings, and it was not until we had used the church and buildings at Ekowe as fortifications, that Cetewayo ordered the Kwamagwaza mission station to be destroyed. The bell in its wooden belfry alone stands intact, all the buildings being completely demolished.

The remark being frequently, though carelessly and inaccurately made, that Government officials, soldiers, and civil servants are opposed to mission work and charge its agents with mischief. making, I think it well to quote some recent and weighty utterances upon this subject which must carry conviction.

Sir H. Barkly, Her Majesty's late High Commissioner at the Cape, said lately at a public meeting in London:

> By the Bloemfontein (Orange Free State) mission, more has been done to maintain friendly relations with the authorities in that state than any consul. Government agent, or ministers plenipotentiary could ever have done.

Sir Bartle Frere, Her Majesty's High Commissioner, who followed Sir H. Barkly at the Cape, said lately at a meeting of the Royal Colonial Institute in London:

I have rarely seen or heard of a mission station in South Africa which did not by its measure of success fully justify the means employed to carry it on. The least efficient missionary institution I have seen is far superior as an agent for civilising and raising the natives to anything that could be devised by the unassisted secular power of the Government.

There are not many English people who are aware that through the Zulu campaign a native contingent of Christian Zulu *Kafirs*, from the great mission settlement of Edendale, near Maritzburg in Natal, fought side by side with British troops, and rendered us the greatest service. The retreat across the Buffalo River, below Rorke's Drift, was covered by men of this contingent. At the conclusion of this war they erected upon the mission station at Edendale a monument in memory of their comrades who fell during the campaign. The Christians of the settlement invited Sir Garnet Wolseley and Sir Henry Bulwer, the Governor of Natal, to be present at the unveiling of this monument. Sir Garnet Wolseley spoke as fellows upon the occasion:—

It affords me the greatest pleasure and satisfaction to be here today, and to take part in this solemn but very interesting ceremony. I am glad of the privilege afforded me, not only as Her Majesty's representative, but as a soldier anxious to do everything to commemorate the deeds of those who have fallen in the service of their country. It is not necessary for me to recapitulate the services performed by the men in whose honour this monument has been erected. Your excellent minister has already described the services performed by the men referred to.

This monument must hereafter be looked upon by all who see it, not only as a record of the gallant deeds of those who erected it, but also as a lasting denial of the statements one so frequently hears made, that Christianity interferes or disagrees with the martial spirit of a native race, or that it deteriorates them as soldiers. In future those who would assert that the native converted under Christianity is thereby injured socially or physically, either as a citizen or as a soldier, must come to Edendale and see this monument, and see the prosperous condition this village has attained.

I have heard it said that Cetewayo frequently asserted that a Zulu made a Christian was a Zulu spoiled, and that the day he became a Christian he was useless as a soldier. I have only to appeal to the history of the late war to prove how untrue this statement in regard to the native races is. I would appeal to all those gallant officers who had the good fortune to be associated with, these Edendale men to come forward and say how well those men fought. In all the great events of the late war, at Isandhlwana, at Kambula, and at Ulundi the men of this village behaved in a manner which was the admiration of all who had witnessed them.

Under such men as the late Captain Durnford, and under those officers like Captain Shepstone (whom I see here) whose dash could never be exceeded, the men of Edendale proved themselves to be worthy of standing shoulder to shoulder with the best soldier of the British army. . . . Wherever the history of the Zulu war is read, the deeds of the Edendale men will be recorded. . . . I look forward to the day, and I hope it will not be far distant, when there may be established throughout the length and breadth of Zululand mission stations as successful and prosperous as this at which we are now gathered. I feel that if the people of Zululand are left alone to manage their own affairs, this will be so, and I can see no reason why Christianity, in the spread of which I take as deep an interest as any man in this or any other country, should not be as great there as in this Colony.

Sir H. Bulwer, the Governor of Natal, who followed, said:—

When I was amongst you last time on August 12, at the public entertainment that was given to welcome back the Edendale troop, I heard from Captain Shepstone who had under his command a number of Edendale men and who saw a great deal of what they did in Zululand . . . a testimony that made a great impression upon me. I heard him say that all the men of the Edendale troop, throughout the war, in the field, in the face of the enemy, even on the day of battle, used to meet together morning and evening to pray after the fashion of the people they had left behind.

He told us that this was not done ostentatiously, but quietly and soberly, and he told us, moreover, that the conduct of these men, their lives, their behaviour, in the field and in the camp, was a living testimony of the sincerity of their profession. For

177

the good service rendered by this troop, and their good conduct in the field, and their good conduct throughout the war, which was almost without reproach, I have already, on the part of this Government and of this Colony, given them my thanks. I can assuredly say that their conduct has not and never will be forgotten by the people of this Colony.

In addition to this testimony as to the value of mission work, .we must not forget that Mr. Stanley, the American traveller, was so deeply impressed with the necessity for missionary effort in Africa, that he not only endeavoured himself, by patient teaching, to convert Mtesa King of Uganda to Christianity, but upon his return to this country urged the Church Missionary Society to send a mission to that chief's country, which was effected.

Neither have we forgotten, let it be hoped, Captain Speke's rebuke to us when he wrote of these central Africans:

What may be said against them rather reflects upon ourselves, who being better favoured have neglected to teach them, than against those who whilst they are sinning know not what they do.

Most of us perhaps have listened to Commander Cameron's warm words in favour of missionary efforts when he returned to England after his walk across Africa.

What Sir Bartle Frere, Lord Lawrence, Lord Napier, and Sir R. Temple have written in favour of *Indian* mission work, is entirely parallel with that above quoted upon the subject of *African* mission work, and may be read in a small pamphlet published by the S.P.G. Society, 19 Delahay Street, S.W.

Lord Lawrence told us, it may be remembered, that if England had not been ashamed of her principles in India, and hidden her Christian light beneath a bushel, the Indian mutiny, which cost us rivers of blood and two hundred millions sterling, never would, because never need, have occurred.

It is not generally known that the Indian Government, which fifty years ago forbad our missionaries to deliver their message, thanked lately the whole body of Indian missionaries for the great services rendered by their work to the State.

Surely the day is past when we need act as apologists for missionary efforts. These facts speak for themselves; they are heaven-sent messages to teach us that if we would hold not only India or South

Africa, but every other country which God has bid us enter, and live side by side with an overwhelming heathen population, it can only be upon this condition, that we make them what He has placed us there to make them. Christians like ourselves.

Usque quo, Domine?

* 9 7 8 0 8 5 7 0 6 8 3 9 2 *